TRAVEL GUIDE TO CHENNAI 2023

An itinerary guide to Chennai's exploration, food, top hidden gems, in 2023

Dan C. Bernardi

Copyright 2023, Dan C.Bernardi.

All rights reserved!
No part of this book may be reproduced, stored in a retrieval system, or transmitted in any form or by any means, electronic, mechanical, photocopying, or otherwise, without prior written permission of the copyright owner.

TABLE OF CONTENTS

INTRODUCTION

An overview of Chennai
History and culture of Chennai
Climatic Factors
Geography

TRAVELING TO CHENNAI IN 2023
Why choose Chennai?

A perfect way to plan your trip
Transportation
Safety and Health Tips
Easy Chennai's Laws to note
Lodging in Chennai 2023

LANGUAGES
The official Language of Chennai

Common phrases in Chennai 2023

EXPLORING

Exploring Chennai's neighborhoods

Popular Attractions in Chennai
Hidden gems in Chennai
Festive Seasons
Chennai's dining and drinking in 2023
Shopping in Chennai
Chennai's nightlife in 2023
A day and a night experience in Chennai
A short trip from Chennai

LEAVING CHENNAI
Practical advice from travelers to and from Chennai
A love letter to Chennai

BONUSES
Bonus 1: Travel quotes
Bonus 2: Chennai on a map

INTRODUCTION

Thank you for visiting the "Travel Guide to Chennai 2023." This thorough book is intended to be your ideal travel companion while you visit Chennai, a dynamic city widely referred to as the cultural center of South India. Chennai has something special in store for everyone, regardless of whether you're a seasoned traveler or a first-time visitor.

We will take you on a tour of Chennai's fascinating history, varied culture, magnificent scenery, and alluring attractions in this book. You'll explore the city's colorful neighborhoods, learn about its hidden gems, and feel the friendliness and kindness of its residents.

We'll provide you some useful advice on visiting Chennai in 2023 before you start your vacation. We can help you with anything from picking Chennai as your destination to organizing your vacation and utilizing the city's transportation system. For a seamless and comfortable voyage, we'll also impart helpful knowledge about safety, health, and local legislation.

Understanding and relating to the local culture both heavily rely on language. You can learn Chennai's official language and a number of useful phrases in the Languages area to improve your vacation experience and converse with locals.

Prepare to experience Chennai in all its splendor. We'll lead you to the city's well-known sights, show you around its fascinating districts, and let you in on the best-kept secrets that only locals are privy to. Chennai has it all, whether you're fascinated by historic sites, curious about old temples, or just want to revel in the city's delectable cuisine.

As dusk falls, Chennai's thriving nightlife comes to life. In the Dining, Drinking, and Nightlife area, learn where to relax, listen to live music, and eat wonderful food. And don't forget to immerse yourself in the city's holiday celebrations, where you'll see vibrant parties and discover Chennai in all its glory.

If you're seeking to travel outside of Chennai, we'll offer suggestions for quick excursions that will let you see more of the area and make your trip more exciting. Additionally, you'll get helpful tips from other tourists who have visited Chennai personally, ensuring that you get the most out of your trip in this fascinating city.

We cordially ask you to read our emotional love letter to Chennai as you say goodbye to it. It is an ode to the memories created, the friendships built, and the imprint Chennai left on everyone who visits.

Travel quotations that will inspire you further and serve as a reminder of the delights that lie ahead are sprinkled throughout the book.

Check out the location of Chennai on the bonus map before starting your Chennai excursion.

Make yourself familiar with the area and let the enthusiasm grow.

Prepare to be engrossed in Chennai's unique fabric, where modernism, culture, and history all effortlessly blend together. As you set out on an exciting journey through this alluring metropolis, let the "Travel Guide to Chennai 2023" serve as your compass.

AN OVERVIEW OF CHENNAI

The capital of the Indian province of Tamil Nadu, Chennai, is a bustling metropolis that combines history, culture, and modernity. Chennai, which is located on the Bay of Bengal's Coromandel Coast, has a long and illustrious history that extends back more than 400 years. Chennai has transformed from a little fishing village to a significant center of culture, commerce, and education. As a result, it attracts tourists from all over the world.

The city's cultural legacy is firmly anchored in its Dravidian past and influenced by a number of former regional kingdoms. Empires like the Cholas, the Pallavas, and the Vijayanagara Empire rose and fell in Chennai, leaving behind an incredible architectural heritage.

In the surrounding city of Mahabalipuram, temples like the Kapaleeshwarar Temple,

Parthasarathy Temple, and the famous Shore Temple are examples of the elaborate craftsmanship and devotion of earlier times.

Chennai's appeal may be found in both its thriving neighborhoods and its historical landmarks. Each area in Chennai has a distinct personality, from the busy streets of George Town, known for its markets and colonial-era architecture, to the calm alleyways of Mylapore, a center of culture and religion. A favorite destination for both locals and visitors, Marina Beach is one of the longest urban beaches in the world and provides a gorgeous location to unwind and take in the coastal scenery.

The monsoon winds have an impact on the city's climate, causing hot, humid summers and moderate winters. However, the coastal setting offers a cool sea wind that brightens the environment in general. The varied terrain of Chennai includes both the coastal plains and the adjoining Eastern Ghats hills, providing opportunity for adventurers and nature lovers to explore the area's picturesque surroundings.

The city of Chennai offers a wide range of activities and attractions for visitors. By visiting the city's museums, art galleries, and cultural centers, visitors may dig into its rich cultural tapestry. The Government Museum, DakshinaChitra, and Kalakshetra Foundation are just a few locations where traditional performances, art, and history come together.

The culinary scene in Chennai is a delicious combination of tastes that highlights the city's varied influences. Chennai's culinary options are a pleasure for the taste buds, ranging from flavorful Chettinad cuisine and crispy dosas at traditional South Indian eateries to aromatic filter coffee and aromatic dosas. The city is also renowned for its street food scene, where lively food booths and cafés serve up regional specialties like masala dosa, biryani made in the style of Chennai, and mouthwatering chaat.

As they explore Chennai's colorful markets and shopping areas, shoppers will find themselves in a shopping heaven. There is something for every taste and budget, from the thriving T. Nagar, known for its silk sarees and jewelry, to the chic boutiques and designer stores in Nungambakkam and Adyar. The shopping scene in Chennai is a lovely fusion of traditional craftsmanship and contemporary retail, providing a special chance to bring a bit of the city's culture home.

As dusk strikes, Chennai's thriving nightlife scene comes to life. The city has a variety of entertainment alternatives, from hip clubs and lounges to live music venues and cultural events. Visitors can immerse themselves in classical performances, concerts of modern music, and the upbeat beats of Kollywood, the Tamil film industry. Music and dance are fundamental to Chennai's culture.

Chennai acts as a gateway to a number of fascinating places outside the municipal limits. Visitors can discover historic rock-cut temples and take in the seaside charm of this UNESCO World Heritage Site by making a quick trip to Mahabalipuram. Another well-liked location that can be reached easily from Chennai is Pondicherry, which is renowned for its French colonial influence and tranquil beaches. Kanchipuram, a temple town famous for its magnificent silk saris and historic temples, provides a window into Tamil Nadu's spiritual past.

Chennai becomes easily accessible and well-connected in 2023. The city boasts a well-developed transportation infrastructure that makes it simple to move around and explore, including an international airport, rail terminals, and a vast network of buses and metro trains. To make the most of your vacation, it is essential to organize your trip in advance, taking into account the weather and festivals.

Any traveler must take into account safety and health, and Chennai takes pleasure in providing a safe atmosphere for guests. It is advised to follow fundamental safety procedures, bring any necessary medications, and purchase travel insurance. It can also be helpful to become familiar with Chennai's local laws and customs to make sure your visit is respectful and easy-going.

Chennai offers a variety of lodging options to suit a variety of tastes and budgets. The city offers several options for a comfortable stay, from opulent hotels and resorts to affordable guesthouses and homestays. It's a good idea to make your hotel reservations in advance, especially during popular travel times and festivals.

Numerous religious and cultural festivals are held in Chennai throughout the year, adding to the city's overall liveliness. The city celebrates its traditions wholeheartedly, from the raucous celebrations of Pongal, the harvest festival, to the opulent processions of Vinayaka Chaturthi. An exceptional chance to witness Chennai's rich cultural heritage and the joyful mood of the residents is provided by these festive seasons.

We'll take you on a tour of Chennai's neighborhoods, well-known sights, undiscovered gems, and thriving food and nightlife scenes in the chapters that follow. You'll learn about the city's festivities, find out where to go shopping, and pick up tips from other tourists who have been to Chennai previously.

Prepare yourself to travel to Chennai for a memorable vacation. Chennai has much to offer everyone, whether you're fascinated by history, art, cuisine, or you just want to take in the lively ambiance of the city. As you traverse the busy streets, sample the cuisine, and make lifelong memories in the cultural center of South India, let this travel guide be your traveling companion.

HISTORY AND CULTURE OF CHENNAI

Chennai, originally known as Madras, has a long and rich past that has shaped its lively culture and sense of identity. The city's architectural legacy, customs, and social fabric have been shaped by the rise and fall of numerous dynasties and colonial powers.

Chennai's earliest known history begins in the first century CE, when it was a significant trading center for goods between the Roman Empire and the South Indian kingdoms. Due to its advantageous location on the Coromandel Coast, the city became a major hub for marine trade, drawing traders from all over the world.

Chennai was governed by the Pallavas, Cholas, and afterwards the Vijayanagara Empire during the Middle Ages. These dynasties had a profound influence on the area, as seen by the spectacular temples and engineering feats that are still standing today. The historic temples of Chennai, like the Parthasarathy Temple and the Kapaleeshwarar Temple, are excellent examples of the elaborate Dravidian architecture and religious zeal that have long characterized the city's cultural milieu.

With the entry of the Portuguese in the 16th century, followed by the Dutch and the British, Chennai witnessed tremendous changes. In 1639, the British East India Company founded a town in Chennai, which gradually developed into the modern-day city. Chennai still bears the unmistakable imprint of British colonial control in terms of its architectural landmarks, educational facilities, and office structures.

Chennai flourished as a significant hub for trade, business, and education under British patronage. The city was chosen to serve as the Madras Presidency's capital, which included much of South India. The renowned Madras High Court, known for its Indo-Saracenic design, and Fort St. George, the first British bastion in India, are two examples of buildings that show the influence of British architecture.

The fight for Indian freedom saw a big contribution from Chennai. It was a hub of political activism and the scene of significant independence movement events. Nationalism was sparked among the inhabitants of Chennai by leaders like Mahatma Gandhi and Subhas Chandra Bose who spoke at events and led movements.

Chennai's culture is a fabric made of several elements that reflects the varied heritage of its inhabitants. Tamil language is widely spoken and esteemed, and Tamil culture dominates. The vibrant arts scene of Chennai, which is regarded as the cultural hub of South India, features classical music, dance, and theater.

Chennai is a thriving center for carnatic music, a traditional style of South Indian classical music. Every year, the city holds the Margazhi season, a month-long music and dance festival that draws visitors and artists from all over the world. The Kalakshetra Foundation is a well-known organization that supports Indian classical dance styles like Bharatanatyam. It was established by the visionary Rukmini Devi Arundale.

Chennai is renowned for its love of movies. The Tamil film industry, often known as Kollywood, has a devoted following and annually produces a sizable number of films. The city's movie theaters are recognizable icons where crowds go to watch the newest films and celebrate the extravagant Indian film industry.

Hinduism is the most prevalent religion among Chennai residents, and religion plays a crucial role in their daily lives. Temples honoring numerous deities are scattered around the city, drawing both worshippers and visitors. With stunning cathedrals like the San Thome Basilica, which is thought to be the resting site of the apostle St. Thomas, Christianity is also very prevalent.

The festivals and celebrations in Chennai further strengthen its cultural identity. The harvest festival known as Pongal is widely observed and serves to highlight the area's agricultural heritage. Chennai comes alive with vibrant decorations, ethnic music, and delectable feasts during the Tamil New Year, or Puthandu. In addition, the city observes religious holidays like Diwali, Eid, Christmas, and Navratri, emphasizing the peaceful coexistence of various religions and cultures.

The eclectic legacy of Chennai is delightfully reflected in the city's gastronomic scene. The region is renowned for its delicious, authentic South Indian food, which features a variety of flavors from sour, tamarind-based dishes to fiery curries and fragrant rice dishes. Idli and dosa, two traditional morning dishes from Chennai, are best enjoyed with sambar and delicious chutneys. Fresh seafood from the Bay of Bengal, prepared with flavorful spices and maritime influences, is available to seafood aficionados.

Traditional arts and crafts in Chennai give yet another level of cultural diversity to the metropolis. Traditional handicrafts, elaborate stone carvings, bronze sculptures, and handwoven silk sarees from Kanchipuram are prized for their exceptional craftsmanship. Visitors can find these one-of-a-kind products and bring home a piece of Chennai's cultural legacy by exploring markets like Pondy Bazaar, T. Nagar, and Georgetown.

Chennai has a reputation as an intellectual powerhouse thanks to the city's educational institutions, which include major universities, colleges, and research centers. Reputable colleges like the University of Madras, Indian Institute of Technology Madras, and Loyola College draw students from all over the nation and the globe. The libraries and museums of the city contribute to its intellectual legacy by preserving ancient, rare, and historical treasures.

With its skyscrapers, IT parks, and shopping centers, Chennai's modern infrastructure contrasts sharply with its illustrious historical history. The city values its roots while embracing innovation and advancement. It serves as a hub for a number of sectors, including finance, healthcare, information technology, and automobile manufacturing, drawing workers from a variety of backgrounds.

The people of Chennai are innately kind and welcoming. Visitors are made to feel at home and welcome by Chennaites, who are renowned for their warmth and generosity. Locals and visitors can meet up and create enduring friendships at the city's traditional arts, cultural festivals, and social events.

Chennai's character is created by the harmonious fusion of tradition and modernity, where historic temples coexist with modern buildings and a global perspective. It is a city that embraces both its past and the currents of change, weaving a distinctive tapestry of development, culture, and history.

As you embark on your adventure through Chennai, immerse yourself in the city's rich history, experience its architectural marvels, enjoy its gastronomic delights, and participate with its lively arts and culture scene. Chennai is a city that draws you in and makes an impact that lasts, urging you to get to know the heart of South India.

CLIMATIC FACTORS

Chennai, which is situated on the Bay of Bengal's Coromandel Coast, has a tropical wet and dry climate. Due to the city's coastal position, monsoon patterns, and proximity to the equator, its climate is characterized by a variety of seasons and weather patterns throughout the year.

Chennai experiences hot, humid summers that normally last from March to June. High levels of humidity are present at this period, and temperatures can surge above 40 degrees Celsius (104 degrees Fahrenheit). Although the sea wind offers some relief, it is still essential to drink plenty of water and find shade during the hottest parts of the day. It is advised to wear airy, light clothing and to protect yourself from the sun by wearing hats, sunglasses, and sunscreen.

The sweltering summer heat is relieved by the southwest monsoon, which begins in June and lasts until September. During this time, the city receives moderate to heavy rainfall, which revitalizes the land and restocks water bodies. The monsoon showers frequently provide relief from the heat, although sporadic heavy downpours can cause waterlogging in some locations. When traveling during a downpour, it is advisable to have an umbrella or raincoat on hand and to use caution.

Intermittent showers and noticeably colder temperatures characterize the post-monsoon season, which lasts from October through December. Temperatures between 25 and 30 degrees Celsius (77 to 86 degrees Fahrenheit) are nice at this time of year. It's a terrific time to go sightseeing and engage in outdoor pursuits. For this season, it's best to wear light clothing and cozy shoes.

The winter months of January and February in Chennai are pleasant and often dry. During this season, the temperature typically ranges from 20 to 25 degrees Celsius (68 to 77 degrees Fahrenheit). While the days are pleasant, the early mornings and late evenings can be a little bit chillier, calling for a light sweater or jacket. It's a good time of year to see outdoor sites and take in the city's cultural events.

Chennai's weather patterns are influenced by the Bay of Bengal's proximity. Coastal areas are more tolerable than inland areas because of the cooling influence of the sea breeze, especially during the summer. Beaches in the city, like Marina Beach and Elliot's Beach, are well-liked destinations where locals and visitors congregate to take in the stunning scenery and cooling sea breeze.

Chennai is vulnerable to cyclonic disturbances, especially from October to December, when the northeast monsoon season is in full swing. These disturbances may result in delays to daily life and transportation because of heavy rainfall and high winds. During such situations, it is advised to keep abreast of weather forecasts and obey any cautions or warnings issued by the local authorities.

Overall, travelers visiting Chennai must be ready for a wide range of weather conditions throughout the year due to the city's climatic features. Before scheduling outdoor activities, it is advisable to check the weather forecast. You should also pack the proper attire and accessories for the season. Chennai offers a distinctive range of climatic experiences that add to the allure of this coastal metropolis, whether it's seeking shade during the sweltering summers, welcoming the monsoon showers, or taking pleasure in the mild winters.

GEOGRAPHY

The Coromandel Coast along the Bay of Bengal is where Chennai, the capital of Tamil Nadu in southern India, is located. The geography of the city is highlighted by its seaside setting, low terrain, and presence of rivers and other bodies of water.

Chennai is situated at latitude 13.0827° N and longitude 80.2707° E and covers an area of around 426 square kilometers (164 square miles). With an average elevation of slightly under 6 meters (20 feet) above sea level, it is located on a plain along the coast. East of the city, where the Bay of Bengal borders, Chennai enjoys a breathtaking coastline that spans for around 25 kilometers (16 miles).

Chennai's topography is highlighted by the Marina Beach, one of the longest metropolitan beaches in the world. Both locals and visitors are drawn to its golden dunes and rhythmic waves, which provide a gorgeous scene for leisurely walks, nighttime strolls, and numerous recreational activities. Other beaches along the shore include Elliot's Beach and Covelong Beach, each with its own distinct beauty.

The existence of rivers and other bodies of water has influenced Chennai's landscape. The Cooum River travels through the city before draining into the Bay of Bengal. It rises in the Western Ghats at Chembarambakkam Lake. Another large waterway, the Adyar River, also flows through Chennai, adding to the city's allure. These rivers' estuaries provide habitat for a variety of plants and animals and support the environment of the city.

Because of its coastal location, Chennai has a tropical climate. The temperature in the city is somewhat moderated by its proximity to the Bay of Bengal and the prevalent sea breeze. However, Chennai is also vulnerable to cyclonic disturbances, particularly from October to December, when the northeast monsoon season is in full swing. These disturbances may result in brief disruptions by bringing heavy rain and strong gusts.

The city's flat geography and coastal plains offer ideal agricultural settings. A wide range of crops, including rice, legumes, vegetables, and fruits, can be grown on the fertile soil. Agriculture in the rural areas close by is well-known for boosting the local economy and food production.

Chennai's historical and cultural development has been significantly influenced by its physical location. The city has long been a center of marine trade, with its port acting as a point of entry for both trade in products and cultural exchanges. During the colonial era, Chennai's strategic location on India's east coast made it a major commerce hub that drew European powers including the Portuguese, Dutch, and British.

The location of the city affects its connectedness and accessibility as well. A vast road system, railroads, and an international airport enable Chennai to be easily reached from various regions of India. Both Chennai Central and Chennai Egmore Railway Stations are important transit hubs with connections to many towns and cities across the nation.

Satellite towns and suburbs have grown around Chennai as a result of the city's urban sprawl and growth. Rapid growth has transformed areas like T. Nagar, Anna Nagar, and Adyar into thriving business and residential hubs. The city's infrastructure is still developing to support its expanding population and meet the demands of a contemporary metropolis.

As a result of its coastal location, flat terrain, rivers, and beaches, Chennai's geography adds to the city's attraction. The city's natural beauty and agricultural productivity are influenced by the rich plains, rivers, and magnificent shoreline. The city's weather patterns are shaped by the seaside breeze and the tropical environment, making it a desirable travel destination for both tourists and locals. The geography of Chennai, a vibrant and dynamic metropolis on India's southeast coast, has been crucial to its historical, cultural, and economic development.

TRAVELING TO CHENNAI IN 2023

The vibrant metropolis of Chennai, the pulsating capital of Tamil Nadu, greets visitors with its rich cultural heritage, breathtaking coastline, and a fusion of traditional and modern attractions. Everyone may find something to enjoy in Chennai, regardless of whether they are an avid traveler, history buff, foodie, or beachgoer. Here is a travel guide to assist you in making the most of your time in this fascinating city.

WHY CHOOSE CHENNAI?

A unique fusion of history, culture, art, and scenic beauty can be found in Chennai, the capital of Tamil Nadu in South India. Chennai has a lot to offer tourists looking for an immersive and varied experience, from its rich heritage and architectural wonders to its clean beaches and scrumptious cuisine. Here are a few strong arguments for why Chennai ought to be at the top of your vacation itinerary.

A Rich Cultural And Historical Heritage

The city of Chennai has a lengthy and illustrious history. Numerous architectural wonders that combine traditional Dravidian, colonial, and modern forms can be found around the city. The Kapaleeshwarar Temple, a superb example of Dravidian architecture dedicated to Lord Shiva, is one of the famous attractions. For those interested in spirituality and architecture, the temple is a must-visit because of its exquisite sculptures, vivid colors, and religious significance.

The Fort St. George, a stronghold built during the British era and home to the Fort Museum and St. Mary's Church, is another noteworthy location. A look into Chennai's colonial past and its significance as a trading post during the

British Empire can be obtained by exploring these historic buildings.

The lively arts and music scene in Chennai is a haven for culture vultures. Especially during the December Music Season, the city is well recognized for its traditional Carnatic music concerts and dance performances. Traditional Indian art forms can be seen and studied thanks to the Kalakshetra Foundation, a renowned center for classical dance and music.

Beautiful Coastlines And Scenic Beaches:

The expansive coastline of Chennai is around 25 kilometers (16 miles) long, and it features beautiful beaches and breathtaking sunsets. Both inhabitants and visitors enjoy Marina Beach, one of the longest urban beaches in the world. You may rest while admiring the huge expanse of the Bay of Bengal, take leisurely strolls along the sandy shoreline, or indulge in delicious street food.

Elliot's Beach and Covelong Beach are worthwhile stops in addition to Marina Beach. Elliot's Beach, commonly referred to as "Bessei" by locals, offers a calm setting and is a popular location for families and joggers. On the outskirts of Chennai, Covelong Beach is renowned for its picturesque splendor and is a hotspot for water sports like surfing and jet skiing.

Yummy And Different Cuisine:

Chennai offers a wide variety of culinary pleasures and is a food lover's paradise. The region is famed for its delicious dosas, idlis, vadas, and sambars, which are staples of South Indian cuisine. It is essential to sample these traditional foods at neighborhood restaurants and food carts. Try the renowned filter coffee, a robust and flavorful South Indian coffee that is a residents' favorite.

Other regional and foreign cuisines are included in Chennai's culinary scene. Chennai has a variety of cuisines to suit different tastes, including North Indian, Chinese, Continental, and Middle Eastern food. The city is filled with eateries that provide delicious dishes from many different cuisines, making it a culinary paradise for food lovers.

The Entrance To South India

Explore South India's rich cultural legacy and stunning natural beauty from Chennai. You may easily travel from Chennai to other well-known locations in Tamil Nadu, such as Mahabalipuram, which is renowned for its prehistoric rock-cut temples and sculptures and is a UNESCO World Heritage Site. You can also visit the temple towns of Kanchipuram and Tiruvannamalai to take in the splendor of South Indian temple architecture and spirituality.

Due to its advantageous location, Chennai is a good place from which to explore Kerala's captivating scenery, including the tranquil backwaters of Alleppey and the hill towns of

Munnar and Ooty. Additionally, you can travel spiritually to Rameswaram and Tirupati, two well-known Hindu pilgrimage sites that are of great significance.

Successful Arts and Entertainment Scene:

The booming arts and entertainment sector of Chennai is well-known. The city hosts a lot of cultural events throughout the year, including concerts, dance performances, and festivals. The December Music Season, a month-long festival that features renowned performers and artists from across the nation, provides a feast for lovers of classical music.

Kollywood, the Tamil film industry, is an important component of Chennai's cultural landscape. The renowned movie theaters are where you may watch the most recent Tamil films and get a sense of the local film buffs' enthusiasm and passion. A number of theaters and auditoriums are also present in the city, and these venues often feature plays, stand-up comedy acts, and modern dance events.

Warm Welcome and Amicable Locals:

The pleasant demeanor and cordial hospitality of Chennai's residents are among its most attractive features. The people of Chennai are renowned for being kind and accommodating to visitors. Throughout your journey in the city, you are sure to come across warm smiles and sincere politeness, from street vendors to locals.

The people of Chennai take pride in their city and are willing to share their customs, culture, and local knowledge with visitors. You can gain a deeper insight of Chennai's history and way of life by conversing and interacting with the locals.

In conclusion, Chennai offers a mesmerizing fusion of history, culture, the outdoors, delicious food, and kind hospitality. Chennai is the perfect location if you're looking for spiritual experiences, coastal delights, artistic interests, or just a memorable trip. As you discover the attractions of Chennai and its neighboring regions, embrace the charm of the city, immerse yourself in its energetic atmosphere, and make lifelong memories.

A PERFECT WAY TO PLAN YOUR TRIP

It can be thrilling to plan a vacation to Chennai since you're anxious to discover the city's rich history, vibrant culture, and breathtaking beauty. It's crucial to plan your trip methodically and efficiently if you want it to go smoothly and be memorable. Here is a guide to assist you in organizing the ideal trip to Chennai.

Research and Information Gathering:

Do extensive research about Chennai before you trip there to learn about the city's attractions, regional customs, and travel requirements. Learn about the ideal time to go, the top tourist attractions, the regional customs, and cultural etiquette by using travel websites, guidebooks, and internet resources. To guarantee a well-planned and hassle-free journey, familiarize yourself with the weather forecast, available local transit alternatives, and any special safety measures.

Determine How Long You Will Be Staying:

Depending on your interests and the things you want to do in Chennai, decide on the length of your trip. Plan to stay at least three to four days to fully experience the city's top attractions and cultural offerings. However, you might want to think about extending your stay if you want to visit surrounding places or partake in particular activities like visiting temples or going to the beach.

Organize a schedule:

Making the most of your stay in Chennai requires creating a well-organized itinerary. Set up enough time for each of the main sights you want to see, such as the Kapaleeshwarar Temple, Fort St. George, and Marina Beach. Consider the location's opening hours, if guided tours are offered, and any events or festivals that will be taking place while you are there.

Take into account a variety of historical, cultural, and natural sights in your schedule. To learn more about the history and tradition of Chennai, visit museums like the Government Museum and DakshinaChitra. To relax and take in the coastline scenery, spend some time at Elliot's Beach or Besant Nagar Beach. If you have an extra day to spare, consider going to Mahabalipuram, a UNESCO World Heritage site renowned for its ancient temples and rock-cut sculptures.

Accommodations and Transportation:

To ensure smooth transit across the city, research the possibilities for transportation in Chennai. Buses, auto rickshaws, and metro trains are all readily available in Chennai, and they may all be used for cheap and practical transportation. There are plenty of taxis and ride-hailing options accessible as well.

Consider variables like closeness to the city center, ease of access to main attractions, and your budget when choosing accommodations. Budget guesthouses, mid-range hotels, luxury resorts, and boutique hotels are all available in Chennai. Select lodging that meets your needs and offers a convenient and pleasant home base for exploring the city.

Become Fully Immersed in the Local Culture:

Immersing oneself in the local culture can improve your trip experience because Chennai is known for its rich cultural legacy. Participate in cultural activities or music concerts taking place while you are there, interact with the locals, and sample traditional South Indian cuisine at nearby restaurants. Gaining some basic Tamil language proficiency will also help you communicate with people and enjoy Chennai's warm hospitality.

Pack appropriately:

Depending on the season you plan to visit Chennai, pack appropriate attire and necessities. The tropical environment of the city calls for light, breathable apparel, especially in the sweltering summertime. To protect yourself from the sun, don't forget to bring along suitable shoes, sunscreen, a hat, and sunglasses. It is polite and respectful to wear modest clothing that covers the shoulders and knees when visiting temples or other religious buildings.

Keep Local Customs and Etiquette in Mind:

While visiting Chennai, be respectful of the regional traditions and customs. You should take off your shoes and dress modestly when entering temples. Before photographing a person or a place of worship, get their permission and take into account cultural sensitivities. It is traditional to extend a kind grin and a courteous nod when meeting others, or to say "Vanakkam" (a Tamil salutation). Since Chennai residents are known for their kindness, adopting the regional customs and etiquette can help you get to know the locals and enhance your trip.

Health and Safety Precautions

Put your health and safety first while traveling to Chennai. Make sure your travel insurance is comprehensive and covers medical costs. Keep abreast of any safety warnings or travel advisories that your embassy or consulate may issue. Use insect repellents and wear proper clothing to protect yourself against diseases spread by mosquitoes, especially during the monsoon season.

Avoid dehydration by staying hydrated and carrying a water bottle with you, especially in the hot and muggy weather. Drinking filtered or bottled water is advised to avoid any potential stomach issues. Carrying a basic first aid kit with necessary medications and toiletry items is also a smart idea.

Acknowledge the Unexpected:

While preparation is essential, have an open mind to unforeseen events and unplanned discoveries. Allow yourself to explore Chennai's vibrant marketplaces, indulge in delicious street food, and interact with people. Unexpected interactions and chance meetings could result in some of your trip's most memorable memories.

With its extensive history, diverse culture, and alluring sights, Chennai provides visitors with a wide range of experiences. You may make enduring memories and fully enjoy everything Chennai has to offer by meticulously arranging your vacation, immersing yourself in the local culture, and being open to new experiences. Take in the city's dynamic energy, indulge in its delectable cuisine, and allow the friendliness of its inhabitants make your trip unforgettable.

TRANSPORTATION

Travelers can pick from a range of modes of transportation to get around Chennai, the capital city of Tamil Nadu. The city is reasonably easy to navigate thanks to the public transportation system, private taxis, and ride-hailing services. Making the most of your stay in Chennai will depend on how well you organize your journey and are aware of the peculiarities of the various forms of transportation. Here is a detailed guide to getting about Chennai by vehicle.

Public Buses: The Metropolitan Transport Corporation (MTC) operates a sizable bus network in Chennai. Buses operated by the MTC are a well-liked and affordable means of transportation that link different areas of the city and its suburbs. There are options for different budgets and tastes in the fleet, which includes both normal and air-conditioned buses. Carrying exact change is advised, or you can buy a rechargeable travel card like the "Chennai MTC

Travel As You Like" (TAYL) card for simple payments.

Metro: Chennai With its cutting-edge facilities and effective operation, the metro has gained popularity among residents and visitors alike. The metro network provides a rapid and practical means to commute and covers important regions of the city. The stations have amenities including escalators, elevators, and ticket vending machines, and the trains are air-conditioned. The metro provides a dependable and convenient means of transportation from early in the morning until late at night.

Trains in the suburbs: Chennai's suburban rail network links the city to its surroundings and nearby towns. The suburban trains are a practical means of transportation for people who commute every day, but tourists can also use them to travel to neighboring places like Tirupati or Mahabalipuram. It is advised to plan your trip appropriately because trains have numerous classifications, including common and reserved compartments.

Autos: Autos, also referred to as autos, are a common mode of transportation in Chennai. Because of their distinctive yellow and black paint jobs, these three-wheeled vehicles are immediately recognized. Auto-rickshaws are perfect for traveling short distances or for getting through tight spaces where larger vehicles could struggle. To avoid any conflicts, it's crucial to make sure the driver utilizes the fare meter or agrees to the fare in advance.

Taxis: Taxis are easily accessible and a comfortable and practical means of transportation in Chennai. At busy transit hubs like airports and train stations, prepaid cab services are offered, ensuring payment convenience and transparency. In Chennai, there are also a number of taxi-hailing apps that you may use to order a cab on-demand, with upfront prices and the choice to pay online. Taxis are a popular option for day trips, seeing the city at your own leisure, and airport connections.

Uber and **Ola** are two popular ride-hailing services that provide a simple and dependable transportation option, and they are frequently used in Chennai. Through mobile apps, you can access these services and quickly book a cab. The simplicity of cashless transactions, upfront pricing, and safety measures are all hallmarks of ride-hailing services. They are especially helpful for those who aren't familiar with the area or who want a more relaxing and hassle-free trip.

Rental cars and self-drive options are available in Chennai from a number of different vehicle rental businesses if you want the flexibility of driving on your own. In accordance with your preferences and comfort level, you can rent a car with or without a driver. You may explore Chennai and the surrounding areas at your own leisure when you have a self-drive vehicle, which gives you more freedom to find undiscovered jewels and unusual sights.

It's vital to remember that Chennai, especially in the center, endures severe traffic congestion during peak hours. Consider the distance, the hour of the day, and the form of transportation that best meets your needs as you make your travel arrangements. Here are a few more pointers to help you navigate Chennai's transit system more easily:

Timing: If at all possible, avoid traveling during peak hours in Chennai due to the city's heavy traffic. The city is generally less congested early in the morning and late in the evening.

Use **navigational tools** such as Google Maps or regional alternatives to locate the best routes, calculate journey times, and avoid traffic jams. These apps can offer real-time updates and detours to help you get where you're going quickly.

Despite the fact that Chennai is generally regarded as safe, it is crucial to use **basic**

caution when taking cabs or public transportation. To ensure a reliable and safe journey, choose trustworthy ride-hailing services or taxi services. Consider telling a friend or relative your ride specifics if you're traveling alone, especially at night.

Local Advice: If you're unsure about your alternatives for getting around or your exact location, don't be afraid to ask a local for help. The people of Chennai are typically helpful and pleasant, offering insightful counsel and direction to enhance your vacation experience.

Parking: Be aware of parking laws if you opt to rent a car or take a private cab for your exploration of Chennai. There are both open parking spaces and parking garages scattered across the city. To prevent any annoyance or fines, make sure to park in the specified spaces and pay the necessary parking costs.

Women who are traveling should take extra precautions when taking public transit, especially after hours. To increase safety and convenience, consider using modes of transportation like metros, pre-paid taxis, or ride-hailing services. Sit in the backseat of cabs or ride-sharing vehicles and discuss your itinerary with a trusted friend or relative.

Accessibility: Chennai is working to make it easier for those with impairments to move around. Wheelchair accessibility is available in some buses, metro stations, and public areas. If you have certain accessibility needs, it is advised to inquire in advance and make appropriate plans.

Based on your timetable and tastes, think about combining several kinds of transportation as you prepare for your trip to Chennai. Taxis or ride-hailing services provide comfort and convenience for longer routes or special outings, while public transportation options like buses and the metro can be economical for commuting inside the city. Embrace Chennai's dynamic energy and use the efficient transportation system to easily travel the city's variety of attractions, cultural sites, and gastronomic pleasures.

SAFETY AND HEALTH TIPS

It can be fascinating and enlightening to visit a new place, such as Chennai, the capital of Tamil Nadu. Prioritize safety and take the required health precautions to guarantee a hassle-free and pleasurable trip. Here are some helpful safety and health advice for your vacation to Chennai, whether you're touring the busy streets of the city or heading outside to its cultural sites.

Keep Up-to-Date: Before visiting Chennai, it's crucial to keep up-to-date on the latest news, travel warnings, and any particular security issues. If there are any travel cautions or warnings pertaining to Chennai, check the official website of the embassy or consulate of your country. Follow reputable news sources and keep up with local news to stay informed about any developments that may affect your vacation.

Despite the fact that Chennai is usually thought to be safe, it is always advisable to take **security measures** to safeguard your possessions.

Passports, money, and devices should be kept in a safe area, such as a hotel safe. When you're out exploring, take only what you really need and stay away from flashing expensive jewelry or other accessories that can draw unwanted attention. Be watchful in busy places, particularly on public transit, and always keep an eye on your valuables.

Transportation Security: Put your safety first when taking public transportation or calling a cab. Pick trustworthy modes of transportation, such as authorized taxis or ride-hailing apps like Ola or Uber. Negotiate the fare in advance or insist on utilizing the fare meter if you're taking an auto-rickshaw. Sit in the backseat of taxis or ride-sharing vehicles if at all possible, and discuss your itinerary with a friend or relative for extra security.

Being **street smart and conscious** of your surroundings is crucial for travelers. Stay away from dark, secluded regions, especially at night. Keep to streets that are populated and well-lit. In busy areas, be mindful of your personal space and on the lookout for pickpockets. Follow your gut and stay away from people or situations that make you feel uneasy.

Food safety and hygiene: Maintaining good hygiene habits is essential for staying healthy while traveling. Use hand sanitizers or wash your hands often with soap and water, especially before eating or right after using the restroom. Take care with the food and water you eat and drink. Choose bottled water and steer clear of undercooked or raw food. Eat in recognized restaurants that are clean to reduce the danger of foodborne infections.

Sun protection: Because of Chennai's tropical environment, the sun may be very strong. Wearing sunscreen with a high SPF, a wide-brimmed hat, sunglasses, and light-weight, loose-fitting clothing that protects your skin will help you avoid the damaging effects of the sun. When the sun is at its strongest, which is typically between 10 am and 4 pm, seek shade.

Keep Hydrated: Due to Chennai's sometimes hot and muggy weather, it's important to drink plenty of water throughout the day. To avoid becoming dehydrated, consume plenty of fluids. Carry a water bottle with you, and fill it up from reliable sources like filtered water dispensers or bottled water. Avoid eating iced drinks or tap water from unidentified sources.

Medical Precautions: Before your trip, speak with your doctor or a travel clinic to learn about any vaccinations or prescriptions that are advised for visiting Chennai. Keep some basic first aid supplies on hand, including any necessary prescription drugs, bandages, antiseptic ointment, and critical prescriptions. Additionally, having travel insurance that includes hospitalization and medical situations is advised.

Protection against mosquitoes: Malaria and dengue fever are two mosquito-borne illnesses that are common in tropical areas, including

Chennai. Use DEET- or other suggested ingredient-containing insect repellents to shield yourself from mosquito bites. Wear long sleeves and slacks and cover up with a mosquito net at night, especially if you're staying in a place without reliable screens or air conditioning. Think about booking accommodations at hotels or inns that have implemented strategies to reduce mosquito populations, such as installing window screens or offering mosquito nets.

Get Medical Help: If you have any health issues while visiting Chennai, get immediate medical help. Hospitals, clinics, and pharmacies are all part of the city of Chennai's well-established healthcare system. In order to have quick access to emergency contact information in case of an emergency, it is important to carry a list of area hospitals and medical facilities. If you need medical assistance, let your fellow travelers or the hotel staff know so they can direct you to the closest hospital.

observe Local Customs and Laws: It's crucial to observe local laws, traditions, and customs in order to maintain your safety and foster great relationships with the neighborhood. When visiting religious or conservative locations, familiarize oneself with the regional customs and cultural norms and dress modestly. Be aware of any particular rules or limitations, such as sites where taking pictures is prohibited. Keep in mind that respecting the culture of the place you are visiting will help to ensure that your vacation is successful.

Even though nobody wants to consider **emergencies,** it's crucial to be ready for them. Make a note of the contact information for the closest embassy or consulate in your own country. Understand the local emergency services hotline number **(112, in India)** and store it to your phone for easy access. Your itinerary and plans should be shared with your traveling companions or a staff member at your lodging so that they can offer assistance in the event of any unanticipated problems.

You can reduce potential dangers and have a safe and enjoyable vacation to Chennai by paying attention to these safety and health recommendations. Keep in mind that your own safety and wellbeing should always come first, and that you should use prudence and common sense at all times. As you travel to Chennai, embrace the lively culture, check out the sights, and make lifelong memories while staying safe and healthy.

EASY CHENNAI'S LAWS TO NOTE

To ensure a pleasant and hassle-free journey to Chennai, the capital city of Tamil Nadu, it is essential to be knowledgeable of the local rules and regulations. In addition to ensuring a great experience, knowing and abiding by local rules encourages cultural sensitivity and responsible travel. Here are some important statutes and rules to be aware of whilst in Chennai.

Alcohol Laws: Alcohol sales and consumption are subject to severe laws in Chennai. The availability and hours of alcohol consumption are restricted in licensed businesses like pubs, restaurants, and hotels. If you want to drink alcohol in Chennai, you must be at least 21 years old, and you must have a valid ID on you.

Smoking Ban: Chennai has banned smoking in public areas, including pubs, restaurants, hotels, and public transportation, similar to many other

Indian cities. In order to foster a healthy atmosphere and safeguard non-smokers from the negative effects of secondhand smoke, smoking is not permitted in enclosed public spaces. To avoid fines, it is best to follow these rules and refrain from smoking in public places.

prohibitions on Photography: There may be prohibitions on photography in some locations in Chennai, particularly at religious sites. It's crucial to abide by the regulations and standards in each place. Photography could be totally outlawed in some places, while in other places you would need to ask permission or pay a price. To be sure you are following the rules, always seek direction from the authorities or from signage on the property.

Road Safety and Traffic Regulations: It's important to become familiar with the regional traffic laws and regulations before traveling through Chennai. To guarantee your safety and the safety of others, obey traffic signals, cross at pedestrian crossings, and obey speed restrictions.

It's crucial to remember that traffic in Chennai may be chaotic, so it's wise to use caution—especially while crossing busy highways or utilizing public transportation—when traveling there.

Respect for Cultural Norms and Traditions: The city of Chennai, which is well-known for its rich cultural past, has its own set of customs and traditions. While visiting the city, it's crucial to respect and abide by certain cultural customs. When visiting religious locations, especially, dress modestly and be aware of regional traditions. Avoid actions that could be interpreted as disrespectful or offensive, and always ask for advice or watch other people to be sure you are acting appropriately in different contexts.

Conservation of the environment: Chennai has been taking action to conserve the environment, and rules have been put in place to safeguard the natural world and advance sustainability. Use designated trash cans for proper garbage disposal and be sure to dispose of rubbish responsibly. Respect the environment, especially parks, beaches, and other public areas, by not littering. You help ensure that Chennai's beauty is preserved for future generations by being aware of your environmental impact.

Wildlife Protection: Numerous wildlife reserves and protected places can be found in and around Chennai. By refraining from actions that could disturb or harm them, we can show our respect for wildlife and the environments in which they live. Never try to feed or pet wild animals, and always abide by the rules laid out by the authorities in national parks or wildlife refuges.

Drug Prohibition: Just like the rest of India, Chennai severely forbids the use, possession, or trafficking of illegal substances. Drug law violations can result in harsh punishments, including incarceration. It's crucial to put your safety and wellbeing first and to abstain from using any illegal drugs.

Currency Exchange and Financial Transactions: To ensure fair exchange rates and prevent the use of counterfeit money, it is advised to use approved currency exchange facilities or banks when conducting financial transactions. Use ATMs with caution, and only withdraw money from well-lit, secure areas. When making financial transactions, keep your personal identification number private and be mindful of your surroundings.

Respect for Public Spaces and Monuments: There are a number of historical monuments, public areas, and landmarks in Chennai that are significant from both a cultural and historical standpoint. It is crucial to respect these locations by avoiding vandalism, defacing, and other actions that could harm them. To guarantee that future visitors may enjoy a site, abide by the rules set forth by the authorities, such as not climbing on or sitting in prohibited locations.

Respect for Religious Practices: With its wide array of temples, mosques, churches, and other places of worship, Chennai is a city noted for its rich religious legacy. It is important to respect the worshippers' customs and beliefs when visiting these places of worship. Follow the dress code, take off your shoes when asked to, and behave quietly and respectfully. To learn about any particular regulations or practices related to each religious location, seek clarification from authorities or signage.

Cybersecurity and Internet Use: As with any location, Chennai is no exception, so use caution when surfing the web and taking part in other online activities. When accessing the internet, always use safe and reliable networks, especially when making financial transactions or logging into personal accounts. Avoid disclosing private information to unauthorized parties or dubious sources, and be alert for scams or phishing efforts.

It's important to remember that rules and regulations can change over time, so it's important to stay informed of the most recent developments and seek advice from official sources or local authorities if you have any particular issues or questions. By abiding by Chennai's rules and ordinances, you not only secure your own safety but also help to preserve the area's cultural history and advance responsible travel. Cherish the one-of-a-kind experiences and insights Chennai has to offer while keeping in mind the city's rules and customs.

LODGING IN CHENNAI 2023

One of the most important factors to think about while making travel plans to Chennai is your lodging. Chennai provides a variety of housing choices to accommodate various spending levels, tastes, and travel preferences. Every traveler's needs can be addressed in Chennai, whether they're looking for opulent hotels, cozy guesthouses, or affordable hostels. Here is a detailed guide on finding a place to stay in Chennai in 2023.

Luxury Hotels: Chennai is home to a number of opulent hotels that offer first-rate amenities, first-rate service, and a luxury experience. These hotels frequently have large guest rooms or suites, excellent interior design, gourmet restaurants, spa services, swimming pools, fitness centers, and business services. The Leela Palace, Taj Coromandel, ITC Grand Chola, and Hyatt Regency Chennai are a few prominent luxury hotels in Chennai. A luxury hotel stay guarantees a high standard of comfort, extravagance, and individualized services throughout your stay.

Mid-Range Hotels: Chennai has a variety of mid-range hotels that offer a comfortable stay with respectable amenities and services for tourists looking for a balance between comfort and budget. These hotels typically include comfortable accommodations, on-site dining options, WiFi, and other useful amenities. The Accord Metropolitan, Ramada Chennai Egmore, and The Residency Towers are a few well-liked mid-range hotel alternatives in Chennai. A nice stay is available at these hotels without breaking the wallet.

Guesthouses and Bed and Breakfasts: In Chennai, guesthouses and bed and breakfast lodgings offer a cozy atmosphere, individualized service, and a chance to mingle with the people. These businesses often have a more intimate atmosphere and are smaller. Guesthouses frequently offer a small number of rooms, guaranteeing a more individualized and private experience. They are a fantastic choice for tourists who want a setting that feels more real and familiar. Hanu Reddy Residences, Benzz Park, and Nestlay Rooms are a few renowned inns in Chennai.

Budget-Friendly Accommodations: Chennai provides a range of inexpensive lodging options, including hostels and low-cost hotels. Basic facilities, spotless lodging, and handy locations are all offered by budget hotels in Chennai. They are perfect for tourists that value saving money while still looking for a good stay. Hotel Greens Gate, Hotel Pearl International, and Hotel Mars Classic are a few of Chennai's well-liked low-cost accommodations. There are also hostels in Chennai that are geared toward backpackers and low-budget tourists and provide shared dormitory-style lodging and communal areas for socializing. Among the city's well-known hostels are Bunkyard Hostels and Zostel Chennai.

Serviced apartments are a great choice if you're considering an extended stay or would like the comfort of a kitchenette and more roomy rooms. The benefits of hotel-like amenities are combined with the conveniences of home in Chennai's serviced flats. These apartments feature separate bedrooms, a living room, and a kitchen or kitchenette. Families, parties, or tourists who value the adaptability and independence of apartment-style living should consider them. In Chennai, two well-liked options for serviced apartments are Somerset Greenways and Turyaa.

Considerations Regarding Location: When selecting your lodging in Chennai, take into account the area that best satisfies your requirements and tastes. The city has lodging options in a number of locations, including the city's core (in neighborhoods like Egmore and Nungambakkam), the IT corridor (in Taramani and OMR), and beachside neighborhoods like Marina Beach. Restaurants, shopping malls, and cultural attractions are all conveniently located in the city center. Business travelers and those who are interested in technology-related activities should use the IT corridor. Beachfront locations provide a beautiful setting and easy access to leisure opportunities. Based on your schedule and the activities you intend to participate in while visiting Chennai, choose a place.

Booking and Reservation Advice: It is advised to reserve yours in advance to guarantee a seamless stay, particularly during busy travel times or significant events in Chennai. A handy option to compare costs, peruse reviews, and book accommodations is through online travel agencies and hotel booking websites. When making your reservation, take into account elements like the cancellation policies, provided amenities, and closeness to the places you want to visit. It's also a good idea to look for any ongoing specials or discounts that could enable you to save money on your lodging.

Prioritize safety and security when making your lodging selection. Look for lodgings with the necessary security measures in place, such as

CCTV cameras, secure entrances, and workers on duty around-the-clock. To determine the reputation of the establishment's safety, read reviews or ask for referrals. Use the in-room safes or safety deposit boxes at the front desk to keep your things secure.

Facilities and Amenities: Take into account the facilities and amenities that the potential hotel options offer. Consider your tastes and needs to decide which amenities are really necessary for your stay. Free Wi-Fi, on-site dining options, swimming pools, exercise centers, business centers, or spa facilities are a few examples of what could be provided. To improve your convenience and comfort, find out if the hotel offers amenities like airport shuttles, laundry facilities, or concierge assistance.

Local Cultural Experience: Selecting lodgings that offer a flavor of the regional culture and heritage might enhance your visit to Chennai. Search for hotels or guesthouses that feature local artwork, traditional architecture, or incorporate aspects of the area's culture into its interior design and ambiance. This might provide a distinctive and engaging stay that captures the spirit of Chennai.

Transportation and Accessibility: Take into account how accessible your chosen lodging is in relation to the destinations and points of interest you intend to visit. Examine whether there are any nearby public transit choices, such as bus stops or metro stations, which can make it simpler to explore the city. Check to see if the hotel has easy access to these services if you intend to use taxis or ride-sharing services. Additionally, take into account whether parking spaces are offered at your lodging if you are driving or renting a car.

Customer Reviews and Recommendations: Lastly, before settling on a place to stay, check customer reviews and recommendations to learn more about prior visitors' experiences. Websites and travel discussion groups offer useful data and first-hand perspectives that might aid in your decision-making. Pay close attention to comments on the quality of the restrooms, the friendliness of the employees, the location, and general customer pleasure.

To sum up, Chennai provides a wide variety of housing choices to fit any traveler's interests and price range. Chennai has a wide selection of lodging alternatives, including high-end hotels, budget hotels, mid-range hotels, guesthouses, serviced flats, and hostels. When selecting your lodging, take into account elements like location, amenities, safety, and opportunities to explore the local culture. Planning ahead and choosing the appropriate accommodations can help you make the most of your time in Chennai and guarantee a relaxing and enjoyable stay.

LANGUAGES

Language is a fundamental component of Chennai's cultural landscape, representing the diversity and heritage of the city. Tamil, one of the oldest classical languages in the world, serves as the official language of Chennai and the entire state of Tamil Nadu. However, you will also find a sizable presence of other languages spoken by various populations in Chennai due to its cosmopolitan nature and history of trade and migration.

THE OFFICIAL LANGUAGE OF CHENNAI

Tamil is a Dravidian language with a long literary history that dates back more than two millennia. It is an interesting language to learn because it has a distinctive script and pronunciation. The bulk of Chennai's inhabitants are fluent in Tamil and speak it often. In the city,

Tamil is frequently used in a variety of settings, including stores, marketplaces, public transportation, and cultural events.

English is another language that is commonly spoken and understood in Chennai, especially in urban areas, government buildings, schools, and retail outlets. English has grown in importance as a communication tool as a result of British colonial influence, particularly among the educated and professional parts of society. English-speaking visitors may easily navigate the city because English signage, menus, and communication are prevalent in hotels, restaurants, and tourist destinations.

COMMON PHRASES IN CHENNAI 2023

Hello / Greetings

English: Hello!
Tamil: Vanakkam!
Thank you

English: Thank you.
Tamil: Nandri.
How are you?

English: How are you?
Tamil: Eppadi irukeenga?
I'm fine, thank you.

English: I'm fine, thank you.
Tamil: Nalla iruken, nandri.
Excuse me

English: Excuse me.
Tamil: Thirumbi paar.

Yes / No

English: Yes / No.
Tamil: Aama / Illai.
Please

English: Please.
Tamil: Vendaam.
Sorry

English: Sorry.
Tamil: Maapillai.
Where is...?

English: Where is...?
Tamil: Yenga... irukku?
I don't understand.

English: I don't understand.
Tamil: Enakku puriyadhu.
Can you help me?

English: Can you help me?
Tamil: Enakku udhavi seiyalaamaa?

How much does it cost?

English: How much does it cost?
Tamil: Eppadiyavathu varum?
Where is the bathroom?

English: Where is the bathroom?
Tamil: Toilet yenga irukku?
I'm lost.

English: I'm lost.
Tamil: Enakku thiruttu pogudhu.
What time is it?

English: What time is it?
Tamil: Eppadi neram?
Can I have the menu, please?

English: Can I have the menu, please?
Tamil: Menu vaanga, vendaam.
I would like...

English: I would like...
Tamil: Enakku venum...

Do you speak English?

English: Do you speak English?
Tamil: English pesuva?
What's your name?

English: What's your name?
Tamil: Un peru enna?
Nice to meet you.

English: Nice to meet you.
Tamil: Ungala paathadhu santhosham.

Can you recommend a good restaurant?

Tamil: Nalla sapadu saapadalaama?
Where can I find a taxi/auto?

Tamil: Taxi/auto enga irukku?
How far is it?

Tamil: Enna dooram?
Is it safe to walk here at night?

Can you recommend a good restaurant?

Tamil: Nalla sapadu saapadalaama?
Where can I find a taxi/auto?

Tamil: Taxi/auto enga irukku?
How far is it?

Tamil: Enna dooram?
Is it safe to walk here at night?

Tamil: Raathiri irundha nadakkavendumaa?
Can you help me find my way?

Tamil: Enakku vetri kidaikkalamaa?
What's the weather like today?

Tamil: Intha naal enna mausam?
Can I have a bottle of water, please?

Tamil: Neerin muzhangu vaanga, vendaam.
I need a doctor.

Tamil: Enakku oru doctor venum.

Where can I buy souvenirs?

Tamil: Smaranikai vaangave enga kidaikkum?
Is there a pharmacy nearby?

Tamil: Pinnaala oru marundhukadai irukka?
What time does the bus/train leave?

Tamil: Bus/train eppadi poraanga?
I need help with my luggage.

Tamil: Enakku bag-a padutha venum.
Can you give me directions to the nearest ATM?

Tamil: Pinnaala irukkira ATM-ku thagaval solli kudunga.
What's the best way to reach [destination]?

Tamil: [Destination] poga oru nalla vazhi enna?
How much is the ticket fare?

Tamil: Ticket charge eppadi?
Where can I find a currency exchange?

Tamil: Velaikku vaanga enga kidaikkum?
Can you take me to the airport, please?

Tamil: Ennai airport-ukku kootitu vara mudiyuma?
Are there any guided tours available?

Tamil: Thiruneri padippu irukka?
Can you recommend any local festivals or events happening?

Tamil: Irundha naalil nadakum nadamadum endru oru maargazhi solli kudunga.
I had a wonderful time in Chennai!

Tamil: Chennai-la nalla samayam kaathirukken!
Remember, these phrases will help you navigate through Chennai and communicate with locals effectively. Enjoy your time in the city and embrace the cultural experiences it has to offer!

EXPLORING

EXPLORING CHENNAI'S NEIGHBORHOODS

Tamil Nadu's capital, Chennai, is a thriving metropolis with a rich cultural background and a variety of interesting neighborhoods to visit. Each district in Chennai provides a distinctive mix of activities, from historical buildings to bustling markets and peaceful beachfronts. Let's explore some of Chennai's most renowned neighborhoods and what they have to offer in more detail:

George Town is a charming and historically significant district in the center of Chennai. The earliest British bastion in India, Fort St. George, is one of its many well-known sites. You may see colonial-era relics and memorabilia in the Fort Museum, which is part of the fort complex. Another reason George Town is well-known is for its thriving marketplaces, such the George Town Wholesale Market, where you can discover a wide range of products like clothes, spices, and electronics. The best way to enjoy George Town's busy ambiance and fully appreciate its rich history is to take a stroll around the neighborhood's winding streets.

Mylapore is a historically significant area of Chennai that is well-known for its lively temples, cultural activities, and traditional architecture. The Lord Shiva-dedicated Kapaleeshwarar Temple is a well-known monument in Mylapore. For devotees and architecture fans, it is a must-visit location due to its Dravidian-style architecture, elaborately carved gopuram (tower), and vibrant sculptures. The yearly Arupathimoovar Festival brings processions, musical performances, and dancing performances to the temple. The San Thome Basilica, an exquisite church constructed on St. Thomas the Apostle's tomb, is also located in Mylapore. Discover hidden treasures like art galleries, music schools, and authentic cafes serving delectable South Indian food by exploring the winding lanes of Mylapore.

Egmore: The colonial past and architectural legacy of Chennai are eloquently displayed in this suburb. With its distinctive clock tower and imposing exterior, the renowned Egmore Railway Station is a testimony to the city's lengthy history. One of India's oldest museums, the Government Museum, is also located in this region. The museum's collection consists of ancient sculptures, numismatic exhibits, archaeological objects, and an intriguing natural history department. The Connemara Public Library, which has an extensive collection of books, manuscripts, and historical documents, is located next to the museum. Discover Egmore's green streets and take in the colonial-era architecture's vintage appeal.

T. Nagar is a thriving business and residential area of Chennai that is well-known for its shopping malls and cultural attractions. It is the location of the bustling Pondy Bazaar and

Ranganathan Street, which are well-known for their enormous selection of shops selling clothing, jewelry, handicrafts, and other items. For those who love to shop and get great deals, the region is nirvana. Temples like the Venkateshwara Temple and the Kabaleeshwarar Temple, which are scattered across T. Nagar, allow visitors to see Chennai's spiritual side and witness customary ceremonies. Enjoy the mouthwatering South Indian cuisine served at the many restaurants and cafes in the vicinity after a day of shopping and temple visits.

Besant Nagar is a bustling area with a laid-back coastal air. It is located along the picturesque Marina Beach. With a variety of activities, it is a well-liked hangout for both residents and visitors. Enjoy a leisurely stroll along the beach, the stunning sunset, or sports like beach volleyball or kite flying. The famous Ashtalakshmi Temple, which honors the goddess Lakshmi in her eight forms, is also located in Besant Nagar. The area has a thriving food scene, with several food vendors offering a wide range of snacks and specialties. You may enjoy the delights of Chennai's street food culture, which ranges from crispy bhajis to sizzling hot idlis.

Adyar: An upmarket, green area in Chennai noted for its research institutes, schools, and calm atmosphere is called Adyar. Adyar's main draw is the huge Theosophical Society, which is surrounded by lush vegetation. There are calm walking trails there, as well as libraries and meditation spaces. The area is traversed by the Adyar River, which sculpts a tranquil and lovely landscape. Enjoy the peace and quiet of nature by going to the lovely Adyar Estuary where the river meets the Bay of Bengal. Adyar is a center for intellectual and cultural pursuits thanks to the presence of numerous notable research and educational institutes.

Nungambakkam is a thriving and international neighborhood of Chennai that is well-known for its affluent residences, shops, and entertainment options. It's a hive of activity, with a thriving evening scene that includes a ton of bars, pubs, and eateries. The well-known Valluvar Kottam, a monument honoring the celebrated Tamil poet Thiruvalluvar, is located in the area. The monument is surrounded by well-kept gardens and has Dravidian and Islamic architectural influences. Throughout the year, Nungambakkam also organizes a number of cultural gatherings, exhibitions, and music festivals.

Alwarpet: Alwarpet is a lovely residential area that combines traditional charm with contemporary conveniences. The region is renowned for its stunning temples, like the Alwarpet Anjaneyar Temple and the Kapali Temple, where you may observe customary rites and take in the meditative atmosphere. Take a leisurely stroll around Alwarpet's tranquil streets, stop by the famed Music Academy, which regularly offers concerts and other cultural events, and savor the regional cuisine at one of the area's inviting cafés or restaurants.

Triplicane is a bustling area with a blend of ancient and modern elements, also known as Thiruvallikeni. The famous Parthasarathy Temple, one of the 108 Divya Desams devoted to Lord Krishna, is located there. The beautiful architecture, fine sculptures, and vibrant frescoes of the temple are a visual delight. Triplicane is renowned for its crowded streets and markets, where a wide range of products, including clothing, jewelry, and street food, can be found. During holidays, the neighborhood comes to life as processions and cultural acts heighten the joyous atmosphere.

Velachery is a neighborhood in Chennai's southern region that is quickly growing. It is renowned for its cutting-edge infrastructure, IT parks, and retail establishments. With Phoenix Marketcity being one of Chennai's biggest malls, the area is a well-liked location for shoppers. Along with a variety of domestic and foreign companies, this area also offers entertainment alternatives like multiplex movies and gaming areas. In addition, Velachery is home to the expansive Guindy National Park, a reserve renowned for its varied flora and animals. Enjoy a tranquil getaway amidst nature as you take a break from the bustle of the city.

Discovering Chennai's rich history, vibrant culture, and different offerings is made fun by exploring the city's neighborhoods. Every area in Chennai has its own distinctive personality, enticing visitors with an immersive experience that captures the heart of the city. Every traveler will find something to fascinate and enthrall them in Chennai's neighborhoods, whether they are history buffs, shopaholics, foodies, or nature lovers. So go outside and discover the fascinating tapestry of communities that contribute to Chennai's reputation as a really active and alluring city.

POPULAR ATTRACTIONS IN CHENNAI

Visitors may discover and enjoy a wide variety of attractions in Chennai, the cultural center of Tamil Nadu. Chennai has enough to attract any traveler, from historic sites and old temples to calm beaches and bustling marketplaces. Let's examine some of the city's well-known attractions in greater detail:

Marina Beach: Spanning more than 13 kilometers along the Bay of Bengal, Marina Beach is one of the most recognizable and long urban beaches in the world. The beach is a favorite place for locals and visitors to take leisurely strolls, take in the cool breeze, and view breathtaking sunrises and sunsets since it offers a tranquil ambiance. The many food vendors flanking the promenade offer a variety of beach activities, including horseback riding, kite flying, and sampling local fare.

Lord Shiva is the subject of the majestic **Kapaleeshwarar Temple,** a Dravidian-style temple situated in the Mylapore district. A sight to behold is the temple's imposing gopuram (tower), which is embellished with beautiful carvings and sculptures. Explore the several shrines devoted to different deities within and take in the lively ambiance. The temple comes alive notably during celebrations like the Arupathimoovar Festival, which features processions, musical and dance performances.

The first British bastion in India was Fort **St. George,** a historic fort constructed by the British in 1644. The Secretariat and the Tamil Nadu Legislative Assembly are presently located there. You may see colonial-era relics and memorabilia in the Fort Museum, which is part of the fort complex. Learn about Chennai's colonial past by perusing the museum's exhibitions, which feature collections of weapons, coins, paintings, and historical documents.

Government Museum: One of India's oldest and biggest museums, the Government Museum is situated in the Egmore area. There are a variety of relics, sculptures, archeological discoveries, numismatic exhibits, and geological specimens housed there. The National Art Gallery, which showcases traditional Indian paintings and artworks from various times, and the Bronze Gallery, which displays superb Chola bronze sculptures, are two of the museum's attractions.

The **San Thome Basilica** is a Roman Catholic church that was constructed on the tomb of St. Thomas the Apostle, who is thought to have preached in the area. It is situated in the Mylapore neighborhood. Visitors are drawn to the basilica's spectacular design and peaceful atmosphere because it is a well-known landmark in Chennai. Enter to see the shrine to St. Thomas and the lovely stained glass windows.

On the East Coast Road, there is a cultural heritage museum called **DakshinaChitra** that showcases the many South Indian cultures and traditions. Traditional homes, antiquities, craft demonstrations, and art exhibitions are on display at the museum and offer insights into the area's rich cultural legacy. Learn more about the traditional way of life by exploring the reconstructed rural settings from Tamil Nadu, Kerala, Karnataka, and Andhra Pradesh.

A memorial honoring famed Tamil poet and philosopher Thiruvalluvar is called **Valluvar Kottam.** A life-size statue of Thiruvalluvar is housed in a 39-meter high chariot-like building combining Dravidian and Islamic architectural influences. The granite pillars all around display his well-known couplets from the Thirukkural, a piece of traditional Tamil literature. The monument serves as a symbol of Tamil ancestry and culture.

Guindy National Park is a sizable urban park in the center of the city that acts as a lush haven in the midst of the built-up area. Spotted deer, blackbucks, and other bird species are among the rich flora and animals that call the park home. Discover the park's walking trails, go to the on-site Snake Park to see reptiles, and take in the peace and quiet of nature far from the hustle and bustle of the city.

The architectural wonder known as the **Thousand Lights Mosque** is situated in the Anna Salai area. The mosque, which was constructed in the 19th century, got its name from the stunning chandeliers that cast a spellbinding glow over the main prayer area. Those who are interested in Islamic art and culture must visit the mosque because of its magnificent architecture and serene atmosphere.

Birla Planetarium: For astronomy aficionados and anyone looking for educational opportunities, the Birla Planetarium is a well-liked destination. Regular performances and exhibitions about astronomy, space travel, and celestial phenomena are available in the planetarium. Through immersive performances and interactive displays, discover the intriguing realm of stars, planets, and galaxies.

These are only a few of Chennai's well-known tourist attractions. The city is rich in historical, cultural, and natural wonders that are just begging to be discovered. Every traveler's interests can be catered to in Chennai, whether they be in history, spirituality, art, or simply relaxing on the beach. So, embrace the city's lively vitality and set out on an unforgettable exploration.

HIDDEN GEMS IN CHENNAI

While Chennai is well-known for its well-known buildings and tourist attractions, the city also has some undiscovered treasures that provide special experiences and a window into its extensive cultural history. Here are some of the undiscovered jewels in Chennai that are worth seeing, ranging from eccentric museums and peaceful parks to secret temples and eccentric neighborhoods:

The Kalakshetra Foundation is a well-known organization devoted to conserving and developing Indian art traditions, particularly Bharatanatyam (classical dance) and Carnatic music. It is situated in the Thiruvanmiyur area. A craft center, dance and music facilities, and an art gallery are all located on the property. Visitors can attend classes to learn about the traditional arts, watch dance and music performances, and browse the art collection.

The Theosophical Society is a peaceful haven offering a soothing getaway from the bustle of the city. It is tucked away in the Adyar district. The society is spread across large grounds and includes lakes, gardens, and meditation halls. Visitors can enjoy leisurely strolls around the lush vegetation, participate in meditation classes, and peruse the library's extensive collection of spiritual and philosophical books.

Cholamandal Artists' Village is a refuge for people who enjoy art and is situated in Injambakkam. A group of artists live and work there as part of this artist commune, which was founded in 1966. Paintings, sculptures, and handicrafts are just a few of the modern and traditional Indian works of art on display in the town. Visitors can talk to the artists, see how they work, and even buy one-of-a-kind pieces of art right from the makers.

Broken Bridge: The Broken Bridge is a hidden gem that provides a gorgeous environment for a calm stroll. It is situated in the Besant Nagar district. The bridge is unfinished, as the name implies, and only a section of it is still in place. It crosses the Adyar River and offers stunning views of the surrounding landscape. The bridge is a well-liked location for photographers, wildlife lovers, and anyone looking for a peaceful getaway from the city.

Mylapore Tank: In the center of the Mylapore area, there lies a tranquil and ancient water tank called the Mylapore Tank. The tank offers a quiet setting amidst the bustling city because it is surrounded by age-old temples. Visitors can relax by the fish tank, feed the local fish, and take in the serene atmosphere. The tank comes to life with vibrant processions and floating decorations during the annual Float Festival.

Vivekananda House: The Vivekananda House, often referred to as the Ice House, is a significant historical site located in the Triplicane district. During his visit to Chennai in 1897, Swami Vivekananda stayed there. The home has been transformed into a museum that highlights

Swami Vivekananda's life and philosophy. Visitors can learn about the life of this well-known spiritual leader by perusing the library's selection of books and the museum's exhibits.

Pulicat Lake: A tranquil and gorgeous lagoon on the outskirts of Chennai, Pulicat Lake provides a peaceful retreat from the city. As a habitat for a large variety of migratory species, the lake is a refuge for birdwatchers. Visitors may enjoy the peace and quiet of nature while taking boat excursions on the lake and spotting flamingos, pelicans, and other bird species.

The Egmore Museum Theatre is a historic theater that dates back to the height of cinema, and it is a part of the Government Museum complex. The theater offers a distinctive cinematic experience by screening vintage Indian and foreign films. Cinephiles will find the theater to be a hidden gem because of its old-world charm and well chosen film program.

Armenian Church: One of Chennai's oldest churches is the Armenian Church, which is situated in the George Town district. The church, which was constructed in 1772, is evidence of the Armenian community's presence in Chennai during the colonial era. Armenian and European architectural elements are combined in the construction of the church. This hidden gem's rich carvings, stunning stained-glass windows, and serene atmosphere can all be appreciated by visitors.

Our Lady of Light Church, also known as Luz Church, is a little-known treasure tucked away in the Mylapore district. The church was built in the sixteenth century and is renowned for its exquisite architecture. The church's magnificent interiors are decorated with intricate woodwork and paintings, and visitors can explore them and take in the ornate exterior and spiritual atmosphere.

These undiscovered attractions in Chennai provide a distinctive and unusual viewpoint of the city. These lesser-known sites offer a view into the city's rich cultural tapestry and provide remarkable experiences for the discriminating traveler, regardless of your interest in art, spirituality, nature, or history.

FESTIVE SEASONS

Chennai, the vivacious capital of Tamil Nadu, hosts numerous festivities all year round. During these joyful times, the city comes to life with cheer, color, music, and cultural acts. Here is a thorough overview of Chennai's holiday seasons, which range from religious celebrations to cultural extravaganzas:

Pongal: One of Tamil Nadu's most significant harvest celebrations, Pongal is observed around the middle of January. It symbolizes the offering of thanks to the Sun God for a plentiful crop. Pongal is a festival where people worship gods, create a special food called Pongal (a sweet rice treat), and decorate their homes with vibrant kolams (rice flour designs). People participate in traditional activities, musical and dance performances, and bull-taming competitions as part of the festival, which is observed with great passion.

Puthandu, or Tamil New Year, is observed in the middle of April. It is a time for fresh beginnings and new beginnings as it ushers in the Tamil calendar year. People go to temples, pray there, and greet one another. Mango leaves are used to decorate homes, and a unique meal called "Maanga Pachadi" is made to represent the various flavors of life. Throughout the city, many locations provide cultural programs that include music, dance, and theater.

Navaratri and Durga Puja: The nine-night celebration of Navaratri, which honors the goddess Durga, is widely observed in Chennai. In houses and public pandals, elaborate goddess idols with exquisite decorations are placed. Garba and Dandiya performances, which include traditional music and dance, are held in the evenings. Vijayadashami, when the idols are submerged in water bodies amidst magnificent processions, marks the festival's conclusion.

Diwali: Also referred to as the Festival of Lights, Diwali is widely observed in Chennai.

Bright lights, vibrant rangolis (patterns produced with colored powder), and ornate lamps beautify the city. Fireworks are set off, sweets are traded, and people go to temples to receive blessings. To welcome the prosperity and good fortune connected with the celebration, homes are cleaned and adorned in addition to organizing traditional games and cultural events.

Christmas: The Christian community in Chennai celebrates Christmas with enthusiasm and holy devotion. Beautifully decorated churches hold midnight mass services that draw sizable crowds. Christmas celebrations include nativity plays, carol singing, and festive feasts. A festive ambiance is created by the lights and decorations that line the city's streets.

Festivals of music and dance: Chennai, the cultural center of South India, hosts a number of music and dance festivals every year. The months of December and January are known as the Margazhi season, which has special significance. The city turns into a hub for classical music and dance performances, with world-famous performers from across the nation. The Music Academy, Narada Gana Sabha, and other locations turn into the hub of cultural activity, providing art lovers with a great experience.

The Chennai Music Season, sometimes referred to as the December Season, is a significant occasion in the city's cultural calendar. A month-long event featuring classical music and dance acts will take place. Renowned musicians and singers perform at numerous sabhas (culture institutions) throughout the city, captivating audiences with their prowess and talent. Chennai transforms into a fusion of classical art forms at this time due to the festival's ability to draw music lovers from all over the world.

Chennai International Film Festival: A major occasion for movie buffs, the Chennai International Film Festival takes place in December. The festival presents a wide selection of domestic and foreign films from all genres. It gives indie filmmakers a platform, encourages cross-cultural interaction, and fosters respect for various cinematic expressions. A comprehensive film-viewing experience is provided through the organization of film screenings, interactive activities, and panel discussions.

Float Festival: The Float Festival is a singular and fascinating occasion that is held at the Kapaleeshwarar Temple in Mylapore. The deities of the temple are carried out in a procession on floats with exquisite decorations around the tank that surrounds the temple. The floats' spectacular display is enhanced by their floral and lamp-lit decorations. A great number of tourists and devotees flock to the festival to take in its splendor and spiritual significance.

Chennai Book Fair: For readers and writers, the Chennai Book Fair is a paradise. The fair, which is held every year, features a large selection of books from many different genres, including academic, fiction, non-fiction, and local literature. It gives writers, publishers, and readers a place to interact, share ideas, and delve into the enormous world of books. The fair also features author Q&A sessions, panel talks, and book launches.

The city's vibrant cultural legacy, religious diversity, and artistic enthusiasm are all reflected in Chennai's festive seasons. Chennai offers a dynamic and captivating atmosphere throughout these festive times, whether you're looking for spiritual experiences, cultural immersion, or simply the thrill of celebrations.

Chennai's dining and drinking in 2023

Chennai, which is renowned for its extensive culinary history, provides a wide variety of dining and drinking options. The city offers cuisines from around the world as well as classic South Indian favorites. The dining and drinking scene in Chennai in 2023 is shown in the following detail:

South Indian Cuisine: Sambars, dosas, idlis, and vadas are just a few of the classic South Indian dishes that can be found in Chennai. At nearby restaurants like Murugan Idli Shop or Saravana Bhavan, you may start your day with a classic South Indian breakfast. Idlis and crispy dosas are served in these locations along with savory chutneys and sambar. Don't forget to try the filter coffee, a popular beverage in Chennai that is robust and aromatic.

Chettinad Cuisine: Chettinad cuisine is a type of Tamil Nadu cuisine that is distinguished by its spicy and tasty food. The cuisine offers a variety of non-vegetarian delicacies, such as fish curry, mutton biryani, and Chettinad chicken. In Chennai, some well-known Chettinad eateries are Karaikudi, Anjappar, and The Bangala.

Seafood: Chennai, a seaside city, offers a mouthwatering selection of seafood delicacies. Seafood enthusiasts are in for a treat with dishes including fresh fish fry, prawn curries, and crab masala. To experience the flavors of the ocean, visit restaurants like Marina Seafood or the Fisherman's Fare at Elliot's Beach.

Street food: For food connoisseurs, Chennai's street food culture is a must-experience. A variety of mouthwatering street foods, including bhajji, bajji bonda, vada pav, and kothu parotta, are available in the city. Enjoy a platter of Sowcarpet's hot and crispy bajjis or visit Burma Bazaar for its renowned parotta and salna. Sundal, a steamed lentil snack, and murukku, a crunchy snack, are frequently purchased from street vendors at Marina Beach.

Multicuisine Restaurants: Chennai also satisfies those who want for delicacies from elsewhere. There are several multicuisine restaurants in the city that provide a variety of gastronomic experiences. There is a wide variety of international cuisines available, ranging from Italian and Chinese to Mexican and Mediterranean. Restaurants with a blend of flavors and fine dining opportunities include The Flying Elephant, Spectra, and Tuscana Pizzeria.

Rooftop Dining: Rooftop bars and restaurants dot Chennai's skyline, providing breathtaking views of the cityscape. These places offer the ideal ambiance for a cozy date night or an enjoyable evening with friends. At restaurants like Altitude, Q-Bar, or Kefi, have a gourmet meal while taking in the city lights.

Cafés and bakeries: The café culture in Chennai is growing, and the city is dotted with inviting coffee shops and bakeries. These places offer a wide selection of teas, pastries, and coffee blends. Visit well-known coffee shops like The Brew Room, Amethyst, or Café Coffee Day for a soothing brew and some tasty snacks.

Craft Breweries: Craft breweries, which provide a variety of artisanal brews, have grown in popularity in Chennai in recent years. These breweries develop their own distinctive flavors and aesthetics, offering a cool alternative to popular beers. Beer fans should visit breweries like The Moon and Sixpence, The Tap House, and The Black Pearl.

Sweets from the past: Chennai is renowned for its delectable traditional treats. The city's sweet stores are a treasure trove of sugary pleasures, from the well-known Mysore pak to the delicious Adhirasam and the renowned Jangri. Popular places to sate your sweet taste include Grand Sweets, Adyar Ananda Bhavan, and Sri Krishna Sweets.

Food Festivals & Food Trucks: Throughout the year, Chennai conducts a number of food festivals to honor diverse cuisines and culinary experiences. These events offer a venue to discover distinctive flavors and foods while bringing together a wide variety of culinary vendors. Food trucks, which serve a range of street food and fusion cuisine in a mobile setting, have also grown in popularity in Chennai.

The 2023 dining and drinking scene in Chennai offers a delectable blend of regional flavors, international cuisines, and cutting-edge culinary experiences. Chennai's diverse cuisine scene will satisfy your demands whether you want South Indian specialties, seafood, or other world flavors.

SHOPPING IN CHENNAI

Visitors and locals may enjoy a vibrant shopping experience in Chennai, the thriving metropolis of Tamil Nadu. The city is well-known for its many shopping options, which include anything from fashionable clothing to traditional handicrafts. Here is a thorough shopping guide for Chennai:

T. Nagar: One of Chennai's busiest retail areas, T. Nagar is a humming commercial center. It is the location of the well-known Ranganathan Street, a haven for shoppers. Shops providing a variety of goods, such as textiles, jewelry, apparel, shoes, accessories, and home goods, line the street. Traditional silk sarees are frequently purchased at the well-known Pothys and Nalli Silks, while Saravana Stores has a huge selection of reasonably priced clothes and home goods.

Pondy Bazaar: Another popular shopping area in Chennai is Pondy Bazaar, which is situated in

T. Nagar. It is renowned for its jovial environment and broad selection of stores that cater to all needs and tastes. Pondy Bazaar offers a wide range of shopping options, including electronics, books, and home furnishings in addition to clothing, shoes, and accessories. The area is renowned for its chaat shops and street food carts, where you may savor delectable delicacies while taking a break from shopping.

Spencer Plaza: One of Chennai's oldest and most recognizable commercial centers, Spencer Plaza is situated on Anna Salai. It has a variety of retail establishments, boutiques, dining establishments, and entertainment choices. A variety of branded apparel, accessories, electronics, and home furnishings are available here. A food court with a range of cuisines is also located in the mall to fulfill your appetite.

Express Avenue: In Royapettah, Express Avenue is a cutting-edge shopping center that attracts people who are interested in fashion. It is a one-stop shop for fashion and lifestyle shopping because it is home to numerous domestic and international companies. The mall also offers a multiplex theater, a gaming area, and a selection of restaurants, guaranteeing a full range of dining and entertainment alternatives.

Phoenix Marketcity is a large retail center with a variety of high-end fashion brands, electronics, home furnishings, and entertainment choices. Phoenix Marketcity is situated in Velachery. The large layout and variety of stores make for a comfortable shopping experience. The mall also holds a variety of events and exhibitions, which enhances the lively atmosphere.

Sowcarpet: Sowcarpet is a thriving wholesale market noted for its inexpensive jewelry and textiles. It is close to Chennai Central Railway Station. Sowcarpet's winding streets are dotted with stores offering a range of ethnic jewelry, apparel, and accessories. It's a terrific place to find one-of-a-kind items at discount pricing, especially during the holidays.

Citi Center in Chennai: Chennai Mylapore's City Centre is a well-known retail center with a variety of alternatives for fashion, lifestyle, and entertainment. It offers a variety of dining options as well as both domestic and foreign brands. The mall is a popular destination for consumers due to its strategic location and contemporary environment.

Khadi Gramodyog Bhavan: On Anna Salai, there is a government-run shop called Khadi Gramodyog Bhavan that sells handcrafted goods. A variety of khadi fabrics, hand-woven textiles, handcrafted soaps, accessories, and traditional handicrafts are available here. It's the perfect spot to buy one-of-a-kind souvenirs and support regional makers.

T. Nagar Thyagaraya Road: T. Nagar Thyagaraya Road, also known as Panagal Park, is a popular shopping area with a mix of malls and independent shops. It is renowned for its assortment of jewelry stores, which provide breathtaking designs for gold, silver, and diamond jewelry. Along the street, there are additional apparel boutiques, shoe stores, and cosmetics businesses that appeal to various fashion tastes.

Several antique and handicraft shops can be found in Chennai, where you may find priceless works of art, antique furniture, brassware, and traditional handicrafts. **Dakshinachitra and C.P. Art Centre,** for example, has collections of rare objects that highlight the cultural legacy of the area and are worth visiting.

With its crowded markets, cutting-edge malls, and distinctive shops selling a wide variety of goods, Chennai makes shopping a wonderful experience. Everyone can find something they like in Chennai's shopping district, whether they prefer traditional textiles, current fashion, handicrafts, or jewelry. So be ready to indulge in some shopping therapy and enjoy the colorful retail landscape.

CHENNAI'S NIGHTLIFE IN 2023

The nightlife of Chennai, the capital of Tamil Nadu, is thriving and has grown throughout time. Even if the city's nightlife may not be as active as that of some other large metropolises, it nonetheless provides a wide range of options for those looking for entertainment and a lively atmosphere after dark. The following is a thorough overview to Chennai's nightlife in 2023:

Pubs & Bars: There are an increasing number of pubs and bars in Chennai that serve a variety of drinks and have a buzzing atmosphere. The Flying Elephant, Gatsby 2000, and 10 Downing Street are a few well-known places. These establishments frequently provide live music performances, DJs, and themed nights, which fosters an exciting and lively atmosphere for guests to enjoy.

Rooftop Restaurants and Bars: Chennai's skyline is home to a number of rooftop eateries and bars that offer breathtaking panoramas of the city. These places provide a distinctive and evocative environment for a night out. Take in the expansive vistas of Chennai's sparkling lights while indulging in a superb dinner or sipping your favorite cocktail. Rooftop experiences at Altitude, Q-Bar, and Kefi are among the most popular options.

Beachside Shacks & Cafes: Due to the city's coastline position, beachside nightlife experiences are also possible. Numerous shacks and eateries are open well into the night on Elliot's Beach and Marina Beach. These places provide a relaxed setting where you can relax with a drink, take in live music, or just take a leisurely stroll down the beach.

Live Music and Cultural Events: The music and arts scenes in Chennai are growing, and there are places where live music performances and cultural events are held. Indian classical music is represented as well as modern fusion and foreign performances. Concerts, plays, and dance performances that highlight the artistic ability of the city are frequently organized at places like The Music Academy, Sir Mutha Venkatasubba Rao Concert Hall, and The Museum Theatre.

Stand-up comedy has become more popular in Chennai as a result of frequent appearances by both local and outside comedians. Comedy nights are held at a variety of locations where you can laugh and be amused. Comedy performances and open mic nights are popular at venues like The Boardwalkers and The English Tearoom.

Nightclubs: Chennai's nightlife has been rapidly expanding, providing opportunities for people who like to dance and party late into the night. These clubs play a variety of musical styles, such as Bollywood, EDM, hip-hop, and pop tunes. In Chennai, some well-liked nightclubs are Gatsby 2000, Pasha, and The Leather Bar.

Cultural Festivals and Events: Chennai is well-known for its cultural festivals, many of which last well into the night and offer opportunity for truly authentic cultural encounters. At the Margazhi Festival, which takes place in December and January, classical music and dance performances go deep into the night. Late-night performances and cultural presentations are also a part of other festivals, such as the Chennai Sangamam and Chennai Dance and Music Festival.

Cinema: Chennai is frequently referred to as the "Gateway to South Indian Cinema," and seeing a late-night film is a common activity. There are many movie theaters in the city that broadcast the most recent Tamil, Telugu, and Hindi films. Well-known multiplexes like Escape Cinemas, PVR Cinemas, and SPI Cinemas provide luxurious seating and cutting-edge amenities.

Night food markets: Chennai's culinary scene doesn't end with sunset. Street food sellers selling a range of snacks and specialties make night food markets like the Parry's Corner Night Market and Besant Nagar Beach Night Bazaar come alive. Parottas, kebabs, dosas, and other regional delicacies are hot and savory dishes to enjoy while taking in the vibrant street food culture.

Cafe socializing: There is a developing café scene in Chennai, with many of them remaining open late. These places offer a laid-back and inviting setting for mingling, meeting up with friends, or spending a peaceful evening with a cup of coffee. Popular late-night hangouts include Writer's Café, Amethyst, and Café Coffee Day.

Even while Chennai's nightlife might not be as vibrant or vast as in some other cities, it nevertheless offers a wide variety of options to accommodate various tastes. Chennai's nightlife in 2023 promises to deliver unforgettable experiences whether you're seeking for live music, cultural shows, pub-hopping, or just enjoying the city's gastronomic delicacies.

A DAY AND A NIGHT EXPERIENCE IN CHENNAI

The vivacious capital of Tamil Nadu, Chennai, has a wide range of activities to keep you occupied from day to night. Chennai has something for everyone, from seeing historical sites to indulging in delectable cuisine and taking in the city's vibrant culture. Here is a thorough guide to experiencing Chennai during the day and at night:

Daytime pursuits:

Visit Marina Beach: One of the world's longest urban beaches is the place to start your day. Enjoy the cool wind coming off the Bay of Bengal while taking a leisurely stroll along the sandy coastline and watching the fisherman at work. Make sure to see the famous Marina

Lighthouse, where you may ascend to the top for sweeping views of the city and coastline.

Visit Fort St. George to learn more: Fort St. George is the first fort in India erected by the British. Visit the Fort Museum to see a display of relics, mementos, and exhibitions that illustrate Chennai's colonial past. Don't forget to visit St. Mary's Church, the fort complex's first Anglican church.

Learn about Kapaleeshwarar Temple: Take in the mystic atmosphere of Mylapore's Kapaleeshwarar Temple. This historic temple, which honors Lord Shiva, is renowned for its exquisite Dravidian design. Visit the shrines, explore the elaborately carved gopurams (entry towers), and take in the rituals and festivities taking place inside the temple.

Enjoy South Indian food: Chennai is known for its delectable South Indian food. At well-known restaurants like Murugan Idli Shop or Saravana Bhavan, you may treat yourself to a classic South Indian breakfast that includes idli (steamed rice cakes), dosa (thin rice crepes), vada (lentil fritters), a variety of chutneys, and sambar (lentil soup).

Visit the Government Museum: The Government Museum is a must-visit location for everyone interested in art or history. This museum, which is situated in Egmore, has a sizable collection of numismatic displays, works of art, and archaeological items. Explore the areas devoted to the Bronze Gallery, Amaravathi Gallery, and the vast collection of paintings in the museum.

Spend some time browsing **George Town's crowded markets** if you want to shop. This location offers a distinctive shopping experience, with everything from clothes and jewelry to spices and street cuisine. The famous George Town Parrys Corner, noted for its wholesale marketplaces and busy streets, should not be missed.

Evening Activities:

Enjoy a Dinner Cruise: Take in a wonderful dinner cruise around Marina Beach as the sun sets. Enjoy live music and other entertainment while taking in captivating views of the city skyline and a sumptuous dinner in a floating restaurant. An amazing and picturesque view of Chennai's coastline is provided by this boat.

Live Music and Dance events: Chennai has a thriving performing arts scene, and seeing live music and dance events is a wonderful way to get a feel for the community. You may catch classical music concerts, traditional dance recitals, and cultural performances at renowned locations including The Music Academy, Narada Gana Sabha, or Bharatiya Vidya Bhavan.

Discover Night Markets: After dark, Chennai's night markets provide a distinctive shopping experience. Browse among a variety of vendors selling handicrafts, clothing, accessories, and street food at locations including Parry's Corner

Night Market and Besant Nagar Beach Night Bazaar. These markets offer a bustling, energetic atmosphere that is ideal for an evening of exploration.

Enjoy Street Food: Chennai is a foodie's delight, and at night the street food scene comes alive. For mouthwatering street fare like bajjis (fritters), kothu parotta (shredded flatbread stir-fry), and Chennai-style biryani, head to well-known areas like Sowcarpet or Triplicane. Don't miss eating regional specialties like Sundal, a salty snack made from beans, and Atho, a meal with Burmese influences.

Discover Chennai's Nightlife: To round off your evening in Chennai, take in the city's nightlife. Visit energetic pubs and bars where you can take in live music, DJ performances, and a variety of drinks, such as The Flying Elephant, Gatsby 2000, or 10 Downing Street. Chennai's nightlife places offer a vibrant atmosphere where you may dance the night away or just unwind with friends.

Chennai combines historical allure, cultural depth, mouthwatering cuisine, and a buzzing nightlife. A day and a night in Chennai guarantee a fascinating experience full of exploration, amusement, and immersion in the city's distinctive atmosphere thanks to its variety of attractions and activities.

A SHORT TRIP FROM CHENNAI

The vibrant capital of Tamil Nadu, Chennai, is a great place to start your exploration of the numerous activities and locations nearby. Here are some thorough choices to think about if you want to leave Chennai on a quick trip:

Mahabalipuram is a UNESCO World Heritage Site that is only 60 kilometers south of Chennai and is renowned for its stunning stone carvings and historic temples. Discover the Shore Temple, the Pancha Rathas (Five Rathas), and the well-known, finely carved bas-relief known as Arjuna's Penance. Take advantage of the chance to see the stunning sunrise or sunset at Mahabalipuram Beach.

Pondicherry: Also known as Puducherry, Pondicherry is a former French colony that is located around 160 kilometers south of Chennai. It is well-known for its colonial architecture, serene beaches, and spiritual retreats. Visit the renowned Sri Aurobindo Ashram, stroll casually through the quaint French Quarter, and discover the Auroville International Township. Enjoy the peaceful atmosphere of Paradise Beach or Auroville Beach while indulging in mouth watering South Indian and French food.

Kanchipuram, also referred to as the "City of Thousand Temples," is a city that is situated around 75 kilometers southwest of Chennai. This ancient city is renowned for its magnificent temples, priceless silk sarees, and extensive cultural legacy. Visit the Varadharaja Perumal Temple, Ekambareswarar Temple, and Kanchi Kailasanathar Temple to take in their magnificent architecture. Shop for exquisitely woven Kanchipuram silk sarees and explore the thriving silk industry.

Pulicat Lake: For those who enjoy the outdoors, a trip to Pulicat Lake is essential. It is the second-largest brackish water lake in India and a refuge for migrating birds. It is situated around

55 kilometers north of Chennai. Enjoy the tranquil beauty of the lake and the mangrove trees that surround it by taking a boat trip through the backwaters and spotting different bird species. Look into the area's colonial past by visiting the Dutch Fort, Dutch Cemetery, and the ancient village of Pulicat.

Vellore: About 140 kilometers to the west of Chennai, Vellore is renowned for its magnificent architecture and rich history. Discover the Vellore Fort, a sizable stronghold from the 16th century that is renowned for its elaborate carvings and impressive ramparts. Visit the majestic Sri Lakshmi Golden Temple, which is covered with gold leaf and elaborate artwork. The Vellore Government Museum, which has a large collection of antiquities and sculptures, should not be missed.

Yelagiri: Yelagiri, around 230 kilometers to the west of Chennai, is the place to go if you're looking for a cool hill station hideaway. Yelagiri, which is tucked away among the gorgeous

Nilgiri hills, offers nice weather, a bounty of vegetation, and breathtaking vistas. For a restorative experience in nature, go on a leisurely hike to Swamimalai Hill, take a boat out on Punganoor Lake, and check out the Jalagamparai Waterfalls.

Tirupati: A popular pilgrimage destination and the location of the renowned Tirumala Venkateswara Temple, Tirupati is around 135 kilometers northwest of Chennai. Visitors from all over the world come to this temple to ask Lord Venkateswara for his blessings. Explore the neighboring sights, such as Talakona Waterfalls and Chandragiri Fort, while taking in the beautiful ambiance and religious rites.

Mahabalipuram: Mahabalipuram, which is close to Chennai, provides a rich cultural and historical experience. Admire the majestic Shore Temple and the deftly carved Arjuna's Penance, two examples of the old rock-cut temples. Visit the Mahabalipuram Beach for some rest and to take in the sea views, and explore the Five

Rathas, monolithic buildings shaped like chariots.

Tiruvannamalai: Tiruvannamalai, a holy town famous for the Arunachaleswarar Temple, is located around 200 kilometers southwest of Chennai. One of India's greatest temple complexes, this temple is devoted to Lord Shiva. Participate in the Girivalam, a ceremonial walk around the holy Arunachala Hill, to feel the spiritual energy that permeates the community. Visit the Ramana Maharshi Ashram and take a tour of the nearby hills' ashrams and caves.

Kanyakumari: If you want a more extensive adventure, consider going to Kanyakumari, which is the southernmost point of the Indian subcontinent. Kanyakumari, which is around 700 kilometers from Chennai, provides breath-taking views of where the Arabian Sea, Bay of Bengal, and Indian Ocean meet. Visit the famous Kanyakumari Temple, Thiruvalluvar Statue, and Vivekananda Rock Memorial. Enjoy the lovely sunset and observe the rare occurrence of the sunrise and sunset being visible from the same spot at the same time.

Among the many alternatives for a quick vacation from Chennai, these are just a few. Every location, whether historical, cultural, natural, or spiritual, delivers a distinctive experience. Create a schedule based on your interests and take pleasure in discovering the many attractions in the area surrounding Chennai.

LEAVING CHENNAI

It's normal to experience a range of emotions when your stay in Chennai comes to a close. With its rich history, cultural richness, and gracious hospitality, Chennai, the dynamic capital of Tamil Nadu, makes a lasting impact. Here is a thorough guide to help you negotiate your departure and leave with happy memories as you say goodbye to this vibrant city.

Chennai provides a variety of transportation alternatives to meet your needs. If you're flying out, the Meenambakkam-based Chennai International Airport has good connections to both domestic and foreign locations. Make a detailed travel plan and make sure you have all the required paperwork, including your passport and tickets.

The two primary train stations serving major cities all over India are Chennai Central and Chennai Egmore. To reserve your desired class and seat, be sure to check the train timetables and purchase your tickets in advance.

Chennai is connected to nearby cities and states via well-maintained highways if you choose to travel by car. To get to your next location comfortably, think about hiring a private cab or choosing state-run bus services.

Organizing Your Things: Be sure to pack your things neatly before leaving Chennai. Sort the goods in your suitcase according to what you'll need for the trip and what can be safely stored. If you have acquired gifts or souvenirs, make sure they are covered and wrapped to prevent harm.

Paying Off debts: Before leaving Chennai, take care of any unpaid debts or payments. This involves paying off any outstanding debts, such as hotel and utility bills. To avoid any more issues, go to the relevant offices or service providers and make sure all debts are paid.

Currency exchange: If you still have some Indian rupees, you can exchange them for your preferred currency at banks or exchange offices that are allowed to do so. For the currency exchange procedure, keep your receipts and any identity documents close to hand. To avoid any last-minute rush, it is advised to exchange money far in advance of your trip.

Return of leased Items: Make plans to return any leased cars or equipment in good shape if you rented any during your time in Chennai. Make contact with the rental companies and arrange the return according to their guidelines. Make careful you obtain all required paperwork, receipts, and return proof to prevent any misunderstandings.

Goodbye to Locals and Friends:
The people of Chennai are friendly and hospitable. Spend some time saying goodbye to the acquaintances, friends, and locals you have made throughout your stay. Thank them for their hospitality and the experiences you two shared.

To stay in touch and keep the contacts you've created, trade contact information.

Before leaving Chennai, spend some time recording the recollections you've had there. Take pictures of your favorite locations, attractions, and experiences to document your time in the city. These pictures will be treasured mementos of your trip and let you remember the experience even after you've left.

Reflecting on Your Journey: As you are ready to leave Chennai, give yourself some time to think. Consider the things you experienced, discovered, and learned while there. Think about the cultural exposure, historical interactions, and personal development you've had. Your trip has probably been forever changed by Chennai, and thinking back on these moments will make your trip even more memorable.

Accepting Souvenirs and Mementos: If you want to bring a piece of Chennai home with you, think about getting souvenirs and mementos that reflect the city's character. These could include customary handicrafts, works of art, fabrics, or even regional foods and spices. These trinkets will not only act as mementos of Chennai but also as one-of-a-kind presents for loved ones back home.

Planning Your Return: As you bid Chennai farewell, remember that this energetic city will always be waiting to welcome you back. To experience more of Chennai and its surroundings, think about scheduling a repeat trip. Make a list of the locations you wanted to see but were unable to do so, and add those locations to your agenda for your subsequent visit to this fascinating city.

While leaving Chennai brings to an end a memorable chapter, it also makes way for fresh experiences and travel opportunities. Keep in mind the memories, say goodbye to Chennai with gratitude, and take Chennai's soul with you on your future travels. Chennai will continue to be a treasured recollection in your trip narrative until we next cross paths.

PRACTICAL ADVICE FROM TRAVELERS TO AND FROM CHENNAI

Experienced travelers can offer some helpful tips on how to get to and from Chennai. Following are some helpful hints gleaned from their experiences:

Plan Your Visit Based on the Weather: The majority of the year is hot and muggy in Chennai. Plan your trip for the cooler, more pleasant months of November through February if you want to get the most out of your visit. This will make it possible for you to explore the city without discomfort and to take part in outdoor activities.

Keep Hydrated: Due to Chennai's warm environment, it's crucial to keep yourself hydrated at all times. Always keep a refillable water bottle with you. To prevent any gastrointestinal pain, it's also advised to drink bottled water or choose filtered water.

Dress Respectfully: Chennai is a conservative city, therefore it's polite to wear modest clothing, especially when visiting sacred places. Men can choose light, comfortable clothing, while women may choose loose-fitting apparel that covers their shoulders and knees. Also, remember that it is usual to take off your shoes before entering temples or other places of worship.

Chennai is renowned for its delicious **street cuisine,** but it's crucial to use caution when consuming it. Make sure the food booths you select practice good hygiene and have a consistent flow of patrons. To reduce the risk of foodborne infections, it is best to consume freshly prepared food and stay away from raw or uncooked foods.

Use Reliable Transportation: When going within Chennai, take into account using trustworthy solutions like pre-paid auto-rickshaws or app-based cab services. To prevent confusion, bargain and agree on fares in advance. Additionally, it's a good idea to keep modest bills on hand for tipping drivers and paying fares.

Keep an eye out for traffic: Chennai's traffic can be difficult, especially during rush hours. Plan your trips appropriately, allowing enough time to get where you're going. It is advisable to examine the traffic situation in advance and, whenever practical, take other routes or the public transportation system.

Use caution when handling your personal belongings: Chennai is a busy city, therefore it's vital to exercise caution when handling your personal items. Pay cautious attention to your luggage, wallets, and personal gadgets, especially when using public transportation and in crowded areas. Use money belts or lockable bags to keep your valuables safe.

Keep Up with Local Events and Festivals: The city of Chennai has a number of festivals and cultural celebrations all year long. Keep track of the local calendar to learn about any celebrations taking place while you are there. Being a part of these events will give you a fascinating look at the colorful culture and customs of the city.

Chennai has a rich cultural background, thus it's crucial to respect local customs and traditions. When conversing with locals, keep in mind their cultural sensitivities and use appropriate manners. **Learn the fundamentals of etiquette,** such as how to extend pleasantries and accept or offer goods with your right hand.

Keep Up-to-Date With Emergency Contacts: Before leaving for Chennai, write down crucial emergency contacts including the phone numbers for the city's police, hospital, and embassy or consulate. In the event of any unanticipated occurrences or emergencies, this information may be quite helpful.

These useful suggestions will help you travel to and from Chennai more efficiently. Embrace the city's diverse culture, exercise caution, and create enduring experiences while you're here.

A love letter to Chennai

My Dearest Chennai,

Words fail to express the profound affection and admiration I hold for you. From the moment I set foot in your bustling streets, I was captivated by your charm and beauty. Chennai, you have become an inseparable part of my soul, etching your vibrant colors into the tapestry of my heart.

Oh, Chennai, you are a city like no other. Your history, steeped in the legacy of the Chola dynasty and the British colonial era, whispers tales of resilience and grandeur. Your magnificent temples stand as testaments to the devotion and architectural brilliance of generations past. I have been humbled by the sacredness of Kapaleeshwarar Temple, and the tranquility of Marina Beach has swept me away into a realm of serenity.

Your cultural richness knows no bounds, Chennai. From the exuberance of

Bharatanatyam performances to the soul-stirring melodies of Carnatic music, you have opened my eyes and ears to a world of artistic brilliance. The Kalakshetra Foundation has nurtured and preserved the classical arts, and I have been privileged to witness the captivating performances that emanate from its hallowed halls.

But it is not just your grandeur and cultural heritage that have enamored me, my beloved Chennai. It is your people, with their warm smiles and welcoming hearts, who have made me feel like a part of your extended family. From the street vendors who serve me their delectable treats with pride to the rickshaw drivers who navigate your chaotic streets with skill and grace, every encounter has been a testament to your hospitality.

The scent of your streets, Chennai, is a heady mixture of aromatic spices and the ocean breeze. The bustling markets of George Town have enchanted me with their vibrant colors and the melodic cacophony of traders vying for attention. From sarees to spices, from exquisite handicrafts to intricate jewelry, your bazaars are treasure troves of cultural delights.

And how can I forget your culinary offerings, Chennai? The flavors of your traditional South Indian cuisine have tantalized my taste buds and left an indelible mark on my palate. From crispy dosas and fluffy idlis to aromatic biryanis and spicy curries, each dish is a celebration of your culinary prowess. The local eateries and street food stalls have become my sanctuaries, where I have savored the essence of your culinary heritage.

Chennai, my love for you extends beyond your physical boundaries. You have taught me the importance of resilience and harmony, of embracing the past while embracing the future. Your ability to blend tradition and modernity is awe-inspiring. The towering skyscrapers of the IT corridor coexist harmoniously with your ancient temples and cultural institutions.

As I bid farewell to you, my heart aches with a bittersweet longing. I will carry the memories of our time together, the laughter and joy, the moments of introspection and self-discovery, deep within my being. Chennai, you have become a part of me, and no distance can sever the bond we share.

Until we meet again, my beloved Chennai, know that you will always hold a special place in my heart. You have given me moments of pure bliss and an appreciation for the beauty that lies in the everyday. I will forever cherish the love we have shared, and eagerly await the day when I can walk your streets once more, enveloped in your warmth and embracing the soul of your vibrant spirit.

With all my love,
Your Forever Devotee.

Bonus 1: Travel quotes

"The world is a book, and those who do not travel read only a page." - Saint Augustine
"Traveling – it leaves you speechless, then turns you into a storyteller." - Ibn Battuta
"Not all those who wander are lost." - J.R.R. Tolkien
"Travel is the only thing you buy that makes you richer." - Unknown
"Adventure is worthwhile." - Aesop
"To travel is to live." - Hans Christian Andersen
"The journey not the arrival matters." - T.S. Eliot
"A good traveler has no fixed plans and is not intent on arriving." - Lao Tzu
"Travel far enough, you meet yourself." - David Mitchell
"Travel makes one modest. You see what a tiny place you occupy in the world." - Gustave Flaubert
"We travel not to escape life, but for life not to escape us." - Anonymous

"The world is big and I want to have a good look at it before it gets dark." - John Muir

"The gladdest moment in human life, methinks, is a departure into unknown lands." - Sir Richard Burton

"Life is short and the world is wide." - Unknown

"The world is a beautiful place, and worth fighting for." - Ernest Hemingway

"Travel is fatal to prejudice, bigotry, and narrow-mindedness." - Mark Twain

"I travel not to escape life, but for life not to escape me." - Anonymous

"Traveling is like flirting with life. It's like saying, 'I would stay and love you, but I have to go; this is my station.'" - Lisa St. Aubin de Teran

"Wherever you go, go with all your heart." - Confucius

"The real voyage of discovery consists not in seeking new landscapes, but in having new eyes." - Marcel Proust

"I am not the same, having seen the moon shine on the other side of the world." - Mary Anne Radmacher

"The world is a book, and those who do not travel read only one page." - Unknown

"Two roads diverged in a wood, and I – I took the one less traveled by." - Robert Frost

"Travel is more than the seeing of sights; it is a change that goes on, deep and permanent, in the ideas of living." - Miriam Beard

"The world is full of wonderful things you haven't seen yet. Don't ever give up on the chance of seeing them." - J.K. Rowling

"Travel is the best education you can give yourself." - Unknown

"There are no foreign lands. It is the traveler only who is foreign." - Robert Louis Stevenson

"The best way to predict the future is to create it." - Abraham Lincoln

"The life you have led doesn't need to be the only life you have." - Anna Quindlen

"I haven't been everywhere, but it's on my list." - Susan Sontag

"Wanderlust: n. a strong desire for or impulse to wander or travel and explore the world." - Unknown

"Traveling is not just seeing the new; it is also leaving behind." - Amyr Klink

"Life is a journey, not a destination." - Ralph Waldo Emerson

"Travel is glamorous only in retrospect."

"A journey is best measured in friends, rather than miles." - Tim Cahill

"To move, to breathe, to fly, to float, to gain all while you give, to roam the roads of remote lands, to travel is to live." - Hans Christian Andersen

"Traveling solo doesn't always mean you're alone. Most often, it means you're doing things in your own way." - Unknown

"The best things in life are the people we love, the places we've been, and the memories we've made along the way." - Unknown

"The world is not in your maps and books. It's out there." - J.R.R. Tolkien

"Life is short and the world is wide. The sooner you start exploring it, the better." - Simon Raven

"Traveling is a brutality. It forces you to trust strangers and to lose sight of all that familiar comfort of home and friends. You are constantly off balance. Nothing is yours except the essential things: air, sleep, dreams, the sea, the sky - all things tending towards the eternal or what we imagine of it." - Cesare Pavese

"I travel not to escape life, but for life not to escape me." - Anonymous

"Travel is like an endless university. You never stop learning." - Harvey Lloyd

"The more I travel, the more I realize how much I don't know." - Anonymous

"A journey of a thousand miles begins with a single step." - Lao Tzu

"Travel far, travel wide, and travel often." - Unknown

"Don't listen to what they say. Go see." - Unknown

"Travel is a way to discover who you are." - Unknown

"Traveling is not just about seeing new places, it's about experiencing new cultures and making unforgettable memories." - Unknown

"Travel is the only thing you can buy that makes you richer." - Unknown

Bonus 2: Chennai on a map

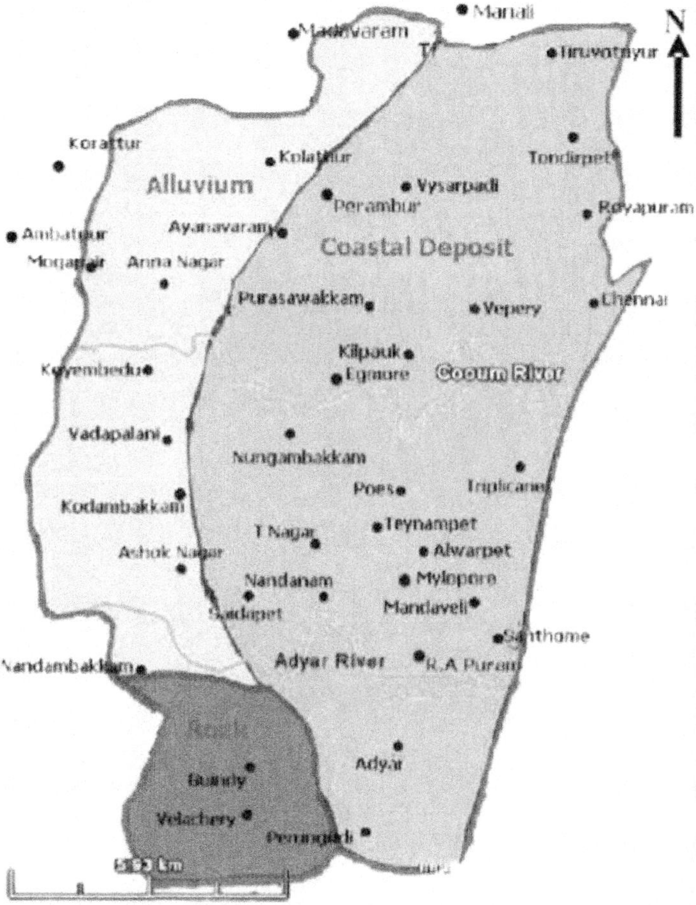
N
Manali
Korattur
Kolathur
Alluvium
Tondirpet
Vysarpadi
Perambur
Royapuram
Ambattur
Ayanavaram
Coastal Deposit
Mogappair
Anna Nagar
Purasawakkam
Vepery
Chennai
Kilpauk
Koyembedu
Egmore
Cooum River
Vadapalani
Nungambakkam
Poes
Triplicane
Kodambakkam
T Nagar
Teynampet
Ashok Nagar
Alwarpet
Nandanam
Mylapore
Saidapet
Mandaveli
Santhome
Nandambakkam
Adyar River
R.A Puram
Rock
Guindy
Adyar
Velachery
Perungudi
5.93 km

Printed in Great Britain
by Amazon